BUDDHISM

FOR BEGINNERS

A Guide to Enlightened Living

BUDDHISM
FOR BEGINNERS
A Guide to Enlightened Living

C. Alexander Simpkins and
Annellen Simpkins

TUTTLE Publishing
Tokyo | Rutland, Vermont | Singapore

We dedicate this book to our parents, Carmen and Nathaniel Simpkins and Naomi and Herbert Minkin, and to our children, Alura L. Aguilera and C. Alexander Simpkins Jr., and to all the true bodhisattvas whose compassionate actions have helped improve our world.

Content

Introduction

The themes and principles of Buddhism are timeless. Over the years, we have all had to let go of much that we had taken for granted. Few of us are given a life of luxury and pleasure like Buddha, when he was living his early life as Prince Siddartha. But we have all seen or personally experienced suffering, illness, aging, poverty and, for some, the death of those we love or care for. At such times, our trust and faith in life can be shaken, and perhaps the meaning and value lost. The philosophy and practice of Buddhism, introduced and communicated in this book, can help us. If we take it to heart our faith in life can be renewed. Release from suffering is possible. When our views change, each moment becomes truly open, new and filled with potential. We hope our readers will join us, to walk the path of Buddhism and to find inner peace through enlightenment.

Buddhism is a philosophy that offers a different way to be happy. Everyday life can be filled with frustration and difficulties. And while we may experience pleasures and satisfactions at times, they rarely last. Buddhism helps people overcome this human condition to find true happiness. Called enlightenment by Buddhists, this happiness is a transformation that takes place within, and is followed by deep calm, clarity of perception, and a feeling of compassion for others. Everyone has the ability to change, because, according to Buddhism, enlightenment is already there, it's just lying dormant and unrecognized.

Buddhism offers a clear method to follow, which it calls the Middle Path. This path brings wisdom and understanding of the source of problems, enabling us to gain control of our thoughts and actions. When this happens, we can recognize things just as they are and understand how we are a part of the whole. When we step out of the shadows of illusion, there is nothing in the way of positive accomplishments or of being who we are. From this new perspective, we can endure and transcend—and live an enlightened life.

ABOUT *BUDDHISM FOR BEGINNERS*

This book is designed to help you understand and use Buddhism as a means of inner transformation. The book is divided into three parts. Part I gives the background and development of Buddhism, to introduce you to the ideas. Part II explains key themes, guiding you along the path to becoming wiser and more compassionate. Part III shows how to meditate the Buddhist way and then how to apply these abilities to everyday life.

You may choose to apply personally relevant Buddhist concepts to your life, or you may decide to follow the path more deeply and comprehensively. Start with where you are. However you decide to integrate Buddhism into your life, let it open your potential to become the best person you can be.

HOW TO USE THIS BOOK

Meditate regularly and think carefully about the ideas presented here—this is the basis for discovering Buddhism for yourself. Deep contemplation will help you understand Buddhist concepts better.

Buddhism is not just a set of concepts or a theory to learn; it is something you must discover for yourself through your own experience. We encourage you to do the exercises. Read through the directions once or twice, then set the book aside and try them. Give yourself time to reflect on the new ideas and skills as you find ways to integrate them into your life. Be patient with the process: The journey of self-discovery may have its ups and downs, but with an open attitude, you will discover your own enlightenment!

PART I

Buddhism in Time

A vision awakens us
From the depths of ancient history
Buddha's enlightenment
Dispels the shadows of mystery
—C. Alexander Simpkins

Buddhist philosophy spans twenty-five centuries, with millions of adherents throughout the world. The journey began in a shadowy past, before recorded history, when a legendary man named Siddhartha Gautama, the Buddha, through dedicated effort and commitment to all human beings, made a wondrous discovery: that life can be good, and so can we. As you follow the evolution, the veil over these shadowy beginnings lifts, revealing a brightly lit pathway of inner discovery, open for all to walk.

1
The Founder Plants the Seeds

Be a lamp unto yourself
-Buddha

EARLY YEARS

Buddhism can be traced back to one man, known to the world as the Buddha, "The Awakened One" (563-483 B.C.E.). He began his evolution as Siddhartha Gautama, a member of the Sakya clan of a small republic in northern India. During this time, India was divided into many small, independent kingdoms, each ruled by clans. Buddha's father was the raja, or leader, of the Sakya clan area, and his family was wealthy.

Siddhartha's gentle-hearted nature began to emerge early. One day, young Siddhartha was playing in the garden with his cousin Devadatta. As a flock of wild swans flew overhead, Devadatta drew his bow, aimed at one of the swans, and shot. The arrow hit the bird's wing, bringing it down. Siddhartha ran over to the struck bird and gently held the bleeding creature until it became calm. When Devadatta claimed the bird as his conquest, Siddhartha refused to give it up. They argued, but in the end, Siddhartha won. He took care of the bird until it was healed and then set it free to rejoin its flock.

Siddhartha continued to remember the bird's suffering. Suddhodana saw his son's mood and tried to protect him even more from anything unpleasant. He lavished on Siddhartha all that he could give, including beautiful houses and delicious foods. He arranged Siddhartha's marriage to Yosadhara, the most beautiful girl in the kingdom.

DISCONTENT

Siddhartha lived happily with Yosadhara, never leaving the confines of his comfortable palace. Although he doubted the importance of the pleasures that filled his everyday life, he continued to feel happy.

One day Siddhartha went outside the palace gates with his servant, Channa. An emaciated man, wracked with pain, appeared on the roadside. "Alms for the poor!" the man called out. Siddhartha stopped the chariot and asked Channa, "What is wrong with this man? Why does he suffer so?"

Channa answered, "This man is ill, my prince. Many suffer from illness. This is the way of life!"

Siddhartha, who had only known good health, felt deeply troubled. They continued along and came to an old man, bent over, shaking, leaning on a twisted cane. "Now, what is wrong with this man? Why does he suffer so?" asked Siddhartha again.

"This man is old, my prince. We all grow old and die eventually. This is the way of life!"

Siddhartha returned to his palace but felt no peace of mind. He could not stop thinking about the suffering he had encountered. All the beauty and joy of life was only transitory! People grow old, perhaps even become sick, and die. Was there nothing more permanent, more real to life? Day after day, night after night, he wrestled with the problem of suffering. Despite his love for his wife and their baby boy, Rahula, he resolved that he must leave the palace to seek answers for his people, to help them.

YEARS AS AN ASCETIC

At the age of twenty-nine, Siddhartha crossed through the palace gate for the last time. He joined a group of ascetics who had denounced worldly pleasures to seek higher truth through a form of Hinduism. The ascetics viewed the human body as the enemy of the soul. They believed that the body could be tamed through absolute denial of physical pleasures, freeing the soul to soar.

Siddhartha found a teacher, Alara Kalama, who taught a form of meditation that attempted to reach beyond the everyday world to a state of nothingness. Siddhartha soon mastered this technique, achieving a state of nothingness, but found that even though he could achieve this state, it did not solve the problems of suffering and death.

Disappointed, Siddhartha sought a new teacher, Uppaka Ramaputta. Siddhartha had heard that Uppaka taught a meditation system that brought about a state of neither consciousness nor unconsciousness. Siddhartha worked diligently at this method and eventually reached this state, but he did not feel any closer to eradicating suffering.

So Siddhartha decided not to look for another teacher and traveled alone instead. He walked southward into the kingdom of Magadha where he met five other seekers. They recognized his intensity and decided to join him in hopes of learning from him. They all lived in the woods.

Siddhartha experimented with many kinds of meditation, always pushing the limit. He tried austere practices, restraining his body, reducing his food to one grain of rice per day. He tried suppressing his breathing to the point of convulsive pains. Day after day he sat motionless in meditation. He endured heat, rain, wind, hunger, and fatigue. He sat so still that birds perched on his shoulders and squirrels sat on his knees.

ENLIGHTENMENT

Seven years passed. Siddhartha had endured the elements without wavering in his self-denial, yet he felt he had made no progress. Instead of finding truth, his mental powers were dimming, his life was slipping away. One evening he was struck with a realization: If he continued, he would die without relieving his people's suffering. How could his mind reach farther?

That night Siddhartha took some fresh milk and rice from a kindly woman. He sat down under a bodhi tree, a type of fig tree known as *ficus religiosos*, that has come to mean "wisdom tree." With renewed strength and hope, he sat down and resolved to meditate until he found the answer to suffering.

As the sun rose, Siddhartha was illuminated with inner wisdom. The answers to all his questions became crystal clear. He experienced a wordless realization, a dissolving of suffering, an intuitive understanding of life and death. He arose radiant and strong, fully enlightened. From then on, Siddhartha Gautama became known as the Buddha.

DEVOTION TO TEACHING AS BUDDHISM GROWS

Buddha hesitated at the bodhi tree following his enlightenment. At first he considered remaining silent. He knew that most people, because they were entangled in worldly attachments, would be unwilling to take his advice. But his compassion for humanity drove him back to the world. After all, he had finally found the answer to suffering. His enlightenment brought him absolute relief and happiness. He wanted to share his wisdom with others.

Buddha sought the five ascetics who had shared many years with He found them living in the Deer Park, located three miles north of Benares. When he approached them, they refused to recognize him as enlightened. From their perspective, he had proven himself too weak to adhere to the strict ascetic path. But Buddha confidently explained his basic insights, and what he said has come down through the centuries as his first teaching, the *Sermon at Benares*. Neither the ascetic path of deprivation that made him sick, he said, nor the way of complete indulgence that made him dull, could bring an end to suffering. He had come to realize that the body must be optimally fit and healthy to withstand the mental rigors required to reach enlightenment. The Middle Way, the path between, was the true path. Buddha laid out the method by which to follow this middle way in the Four Noble Truths and the Eightfold Path (see Chapter 6).

Four of the five ascetics reluctantly sat around him to listen, yet after he expressed his realization to them, they were all converted. They joined him and began teaching his path, thus marking the birth of Buddhism.

Buddha and his small band of disciples walked from place to place, spreading the message and gathering followers. Their days were spent traveling, begging for food, eating, bathing, and then listening to talks from Buddha before traveling on.

On the journey from Benares to Rajagriha, another large city in northern India, Buddha met Kasyapa. Kasyapa and his two brothers were leaders of a large fire-worshiping sect of over a thousand ascetics. At first, Kasyapa did not believe that Buddha held any special knowledge. Buddha convinced him with a discourse that has come to be known as the *Fire Sermon*. The entire group sat together in an area called Elephant Rock overlooking Rajagriha valley. Just then, a fire broke out in the jungle on a nearby hill. Buddha seized upon this natural occurrence to teach.

Like the fire that was consuming the trees, plants, and animals, so our passions consume us, he said. Whenever we see something, it ignites an inward reaction of either pleasure or pain. Our sensations fuel these inner fires, consuming us in a never-ending inferno of desire for pleasure and fear of pain. Buddha taught that the Four Noble Truths and the Eightfold Path free us from these fires. Then we can see without craving, free to be happy. This sermon convinced Kasyapa that Buddhism offered a true path for him.

Kasyapa, along with his two brothers and many of his followers, joined Buddha in his travels. Kasyapa became Mahakasyapa, one of the primary disciples who organized the Order after Buddha's death. Through his travels, Buddha continued to gather followers and supporters from all levels of society. His willingness to accept anyone, no matter what their caste, was a radical departure from traditional Hindu protocol. Usually religion had been taught in Vedic Sanskrit, a language used only by the upper castes. Buddha felt that teaching in Vedic Sanskrit would make it impossible for anyone from lower castes to understand his sermons. Thus he always used the common language.

When the group arrived in Rajagriha, they were met by the ruler of the area, King Bimbisara. On hearing Buddha lecture, the king offered Buddha a residence in one of his nearby bamboo groves. Buddha and his disciples spent many rainy seasons in this grove, and it was here that Buddha delivered some of his most complex speeches. During his first year there, Buddha converted Sariputra, who was later involved in many conversations with Buddha, recorded in the sermons. Sariputra joined the community, called the *sangha*.

Buddha's father had kept track of his son's progress through the years, and eventually he sent a message asking Buddha to make a visit. Buddha decided to return to his home with his entire company. They arrived in a local park and, as was their custom, went from house to house begging for food. The town watched, somewhat horrified to see their prince dressed in simple robes, extending his begging bowl. Suddhodana walked up to his son and confronted him, "Why do you disgrace the family?"

Buddha replied, "Your lineage is of princes; my lineage now is from buddhas who have always begged for their food." Still, Buddha did not want to hurt his father, nor did he wish to show him disrespect. He continued, "When someone finds a treasure it is his duty to give it to his father. And so, I offer to you, Father, my most precious treasure: my doctrines."

After listening carefully, Suddhodana could see that his son was following an honorable path. Without uttering a word, Suddhodana took his son's bowl and gestured for him to enter the palace. The entire household honored him, solidifying their bonds in a new way. Eventually, many of them joined Buddha's group.

For forty-five years Buddha preached, traveled by foot around the area of northern India, and returned during each rainy season to the bamboo grove. Although many people accepted his teachings without question, some voiced objections. Devadatta, Buddha's childhood companion, tried to convince Buddha to become stricter. He believed monks should be required to live outdoors, wear rags, eat no meat, and never accept invitations to join people for a meal. Buddha said this was unnecessary. As long as people were not overindulgent, it was not important where they slept, how or where they ate, or what they wore. Dissatisfied with Buddha's answer, Devadatta founded his own conservative order, and gathered many supporters. Throughout Buddha's career he encountered people who objected to aspects of his message. These dissenters were the precursors to the divisions that would take place years after Buddha's death.

BUDDHA'S FINAL DAYS

During the rainy season of his eightieth year, Buddha became ill and realized that his life was drawing to a close. He gathered all his followers around him. Speaking earnestly, he directed them to continue following the way he had set out so that the teachings could live on. He told his disciples, "Mendicants, I now impress upon you, decay is inherent in all component things; work out your salvation with diligence!" These were the last words he spoke before he slipped away, peacefully. The year was recorded as 483 B.C.E.

2
Buddhism Takes Root

The disciples of Gotama are always well awake, and their mind day and night always delights in meditation.
—The Dhammapada

THE FIRST COUNCIL

The funeral ceremonies began, but the monks in attendance agreed to wait for Mahakasyapa to return from his travels before they performed the cremation. Meanwhile, Mahakasyapa met a group of monks in the village of Pava who informed him that Buddha had died. One of them remarked, "Don't be unhappy. We are finally free to do as we wish without being reprimanded and corrected all the time!" Concerned about the rebellious sentiment, Mahakasyapa hurried back to the funeral site to complete the rites.

Following Buddha's death, many members of the Order dispersed. There was nothing to keep them together. Mahakasyapa recognized that something had to be done to formally set out the rules and teachings of Buddha to keep the Order gathered. Three months after Buddha's death, Mahakasyapa called together the five hundred who remained. They gathered at a place near Rajagriha into what has come to be called the First Buddhist Council.

All who gathered had reached enlightenment except Ananda. Ananda had been continually at Buddha's side for the past twenty-five years and knew all of Buddha's sermons by heart. Therefore, the monks agreed that Ananda should be included at the council.

Ananda desperately wanted to become enlightened. According to legend, the night before the council convened he stayed up all night trying to reach enlightenment. Unsuccessful, he finally decided to give up and go to bed. When he lay down on his bed, so the legend goes, his head mysteriously lifted off the pillow and his feet raised from the bed. He became enlightened.

The five hundred monks spent the three months of the rainy season gathering Buddha's teachings, preserving them in three sections: the words of the Buddha, called the Doctrines of the Elders (Thera Vada), the rules of the Order (Vinaya), and the general precepts for both the monks and the laity (Dharma). Ananda recited the sermons as he remembered them, beginning each one with the words: "Thus have I heard," which is how the earliest sermons, later known as *sutras*, begin.

The entire council recited all the information together to commit it to memory. According to the custom of the time, nothing was written down. Our respect for the written word was not shared by early civilizations. Originally, people believed that sacred words would be trivialized, their deeper intent lost, if they were written down. Important information was best preserved when learned by heart. As a result of this belief, for several centuries Buddha's lectures were perpetuated solely in the memory of the monks.

The monks continued to walk the Eightfold Path that Buddha had shown. Through meditation that helped them recognize impermanence and give up desires, they sought to find enlightenment. They became known as *arhats*, followers of the saintly, noble way, and they lived in seclusion so as to foster and develop their enlightenment. Through deep meditation on the Eightfold Path, they escaped the problems of sickness, death, and suffering. The reputation of arhats as absolutely pure beings grew.

BUDDHISM DIVIDES INTO SECTS

For the next hundred years, differences that had always been present, even during Buddha's lifetime, became more pronounced. Some followers felt that the traditional rules and practices set out by the First Council were too strict. A second council of seven hundred monks was called at Vaisali to resolve the divisions and set down the rules and teachings as they had developed. One contingent of more liberal monks requested what was called the "Ten Indulgences," asking for the loosening of the rules and restrictions on alcohol, money, and behavior.

In the end, the council upheld the conservative version of the rules without change. Dissatisfied with the council's decision, members of the liberal faction, under their leader Mahadeva, held their own meeting, which they called Maha Sangiti (the Great Council). This was the origin of a new sect of Buddhism, the Mahasanghikas, which paved the way for Mahayana.

After the Second Council, the monks continued to wander around the countryside in groups, teaching the doctrine from memory. Each member tended to specialize, becoming expert in one sutra. Inevitably, variations began to occur. People and groups not only lived in different parts of the country, but also learned different doctrines. At first, the groups got along amicably, recognizing that they were simply traveling different paths to the same goal. But gradually, distinctions became disputes that grew more frequent and intense. At least eighteen separate sects formed.

Since all the orders depended on the general population for support, the liberal Mahasanghikas wanted to relax the strict rules about who could be enlightened so that everyday people could be included. Mahadeva argued, "Why not put your faith in the Buddha who achieved perfect enlightenment and remains forever in Nirvana?"

The conservative sect adversarial to the Mahasanghikas called themselves Sthaviras, meaning Elders. In Sanskrit, this name translates as Theravadins, one of the Buddhist groups that continues today in Southeast Asia. Theravadins claimed that they had seniority and were the keepers of Buddha's original orthodoxy. They tried to stay with the early traditions without changing them. To let go of passions, discover wisdom in meditation, and then become an arhat continued to be the highest goal for these followers.

The sects disputed other issues, but the major division was between the Elders and those who preferred a more liberal doctrine.

ASOKA, THE BUDDHIST KING

Asoka, who ruled from 274 to 236 B.C.E., began his career as a military leader. After conquering Magadha, Asoka was crowned king, and each of his six brothers was given his own city to rule. Asoka, however, did not get along with his brothers and attacked their kingdoms repeatedly. Eventually, he was victorious, brutally killing all six. He continued his murderous rampage until the entire territory was his.

Many legends tell of Asoka's cruelty. He believed that the more people he killed, the stronger his kingdom would become. He built a sacrificial house where executions were performed and decreed that anyone who entered the house was to be killed. He was said to have slaughtered thousands of innocent people.

One day a young Buddhist seeker named Samudra, who had not yet found enlightenment, wandered into the sacrificial house by mistake. Raising his sword, the executioner approached the monk. Samudra asked innocently, "Why are you attacking me?"

The executioner explained, "Now that you have entered this house, I am obliged to kill you."

Samudra said, "I will accept that, but leave me here for seven days. I will not move from this spot." The executioner agreed and left. The monk sat down amid all the blood and began to meditate. He could see the remains of the many lives that had been cut short. Suddenly, as he realized the impermanence of all things, he was enlightened.

On the seventh day, the executioner returned to kill Samudra. Thinking of a new way to accomplish this chore, the executioner placed Samudra in a cauldron of burning oil for a whole day, but

Samudra was now impervious to harm. Hearing about this strange event, the king strode into the house to see for himself. The executioner looked visibly upset. "Sire! You have entered the house, and now by your own order, I must kill you!"

But Asoka cleverly countered, "Ah, but you entered first, so I must first kill you."

The monk interrupted their arguing. "I have miraculously been able to endure this burning oil because of my meditation!" In a persuasive speech about the benefits of Buddhism, he urged the king to repent of his sins. Deeply moved, the king underwent a complete conversion. He destroyed his slaughterhouse and put all his efforts into learning and practicing Buddhism.

King Asoka did more than any previous ruler to spread Buddhism. He urged his citizens to follow the guidelines of Buddhism: to become moral, act justly, and live lives filled with love and compassion. People should obey their parents, respect living creatures, tell the truth, and revere their teachers. Not only did he build Buddhist temples and monasteries all around India, but he also established hospitals for both people and animals, and planted gardens. He even denounced war, asserting firmly that the only conquest left for him was the dharma, Buddhist teachings. Asoka's story can be an inspiration to anyone on the wrong Path. Redemption is possible. Some historians believe that a third council was called by Asoka and took place around 237 B.C.E., at Pataliputra, lasting for nine months. Asoka donated funds to allow the Theravadins to write down the sutras and rules of the order for the first time. The sutras were grouped together in the *Sutta-pitaka* (sutra basket) and were actually kept in a basket at first. The rules of the Order were collected into the *Vinaya-pitaka* (ordinance basket). The commentaries written soon after Buddha's death, explaining and developing his teachings, were called the *Abhidharma-pitaka* (treatise basket). The three baskets together were known as the *Tipitaka*, the *Law Treasure of Buddhism*. These texts, written in the Pali language, became the literature of early Buddhism, which included Theravada. They are considered the record of the teachings of Buddha and are the oldest written works of Buddhism. They are separate from the later Sanskrit writings of the Mahayana, done in the first century C.E.

Asoka sent missionaries throughout India and neighboring countries to convert people. Even his eldest son, Mahinda, was a devout Buddhist monk. King Asoka sent the prince and his disciples south to transmit Buddhism to Sri Lanka. Mahinda and eight other delegations spread Theravada Buddhism in the Pali language. It was widely accepted and spread to Burma, Thailand, Laos, and Cambodia, where this form, Theravada (Hinayana) Buddhism, is still practiced widely today.

BUDDHISM OF THE ELDERS SPREADS

According to most accounts, the first country outside of India to receive Buddhism was Ceylon, now Sri Lanka. However, the Sinhalese chronicles and commentaries on the Pali scriptures, written by the ancient people of Ceylon, relate how Buddha personally traveled to Ceylon three times to give them the teachings directly. Early Burmese and Thai Buddhist writings also contain legends, much like the Sinhalese, that claimed Buddha had visited their countries. They believed some of the Indian Pali sutras secretly referred to people and places in Southeast Asia.

Despite these stories, historians believe the first contact with Buddhism came well after Buddha's death, when King Devanamispiya was introduced to Buddhism by Asoka's son. The Ceylonese king liked Buddhism so much that he built a monastery at the capital city, Anuradhapura, and established Theravada as the official form of Buddhism.

Later, King Asoka's daughter, Sanghamittla, brought to Ceylon a branch from the original bodhi tree where Buddha attained enlightenment. With this important symbol of the Buddha himself, she founded an order of nuns that lasted for many centuries. However, nuns were given a lesser role in Southeast Asian Buddhism, and the order eventually died out.

Over the centuries, Buddhism enjoyed royal patronage. The sangha had a close relationship with the governments of Ceylon, Burma, and Thailand. This strong interdependency helped Theravada Buddhism, later renamed as Hinayana, to develop in new directions.

HINAYANA'S NEW ROLE FOR MONKS AND THE LAITY

The tradition that developed over the centuries altered Hinayana's original narrow application as a philosophy only for monks. Hinayana became a large religion with a definite place for the general population. Monks continued to pursue the Path to become arhats. But a new way developed for people to practice Buddhism even if they stayed with their families, owned property, and pursued a career. Hinayana Buddhism guided the general public to live ethical, fulfilling, and happy lives with the promise that they would be reborn in a happier state in their next life.

Goals for the layperson were more modest than were the goals for the monks. First, just like the monks, people must sincerely follow the precepts not to kill, steal, be lustful, lie, or take intoxicants. They also were to take refuge in the Buddha, the dharma, and the sangha. Taking refuge in the Buddha meant they were to respect and revere Buddha as an enlightened guide to wisdom.

Taking refuge in the dharma involved learning about the teachings of Buddha, although laypersons did not go into as much detail as the monks. They did learn about mindfulness meditation and control of desires, but they followed these teachings more moderately. The monks taught people meditation and rituals that could set them on a gradual path to enlightenment. Once a week people went to the monastery to meditate and perform rituals that helped them become more alert and aware, calmer and happier.

On this day they were to eat nothing after noon and wear simple clothes without any jewelry. They sat on the floor, refraining from the comforts of plush furniture or modern conveniences. In a moderate way, people learned to overcome their suffering by lessening desires and becoming more aware.

Taking refuge in the sangha involved helping the monks and the monastery with financial support. When people gave food and money, they earned merit toward a higher rebirth in their next life. Thus, laypersons were encouraged to work and accumulate wealth, so long as their work did not violate the precepts. Commensurate with the amount of wealth people acquired, they were expected to share some of it with the sangha, who relied entirely on the public for support.

Kings, like the common people, were expected to give generously to the sangha, building monasteries and donating financial support. In return, monks taught meditation to the kings and offered an enlightened perspective to help them rule wisely so that the kingdom could thrive.

The close relationship between the monastery and the government put new responsibilities on the monks. The rulers expected the monks to help the people by running Buddhist schools where children could learn reading and writing along with Buddhism. During the rainy season, when no farming could be done, sons were sent to the monastery to live as monks. They shaved their heads and wore the robes. Sometimes they even gave up their regular form of livelihood to join the sangha and become monks. Usually they returned home, but often enriched by the experience.

Hinayana Buddhism is still practiced in many Southeast Asian countries today, where centrally located monasteries are an important part of everyday life. But along the way, Buddhism's path took a dramatic turn as the liberal form developed into Mahayana.

3
The Blossom of Mahayana

What makes the limit of Nirvana
Is also then the limit of Samsara
Between the two we cannot find
The slightest shade of difference.
—Nagarjuna

BUDDHISM EVOLVES

At first, conservative and liberal interpretations were not fully opposed. The monks from both perspectives lived and taught side by side for close to four hundred years. Gradually, though, Buddhist doctrine began to change; by around 100 C.E., a new literature and a new rationale for the dissenting doctrine emerged.

This new literature revealed a doctrine that creatively reinterpreted the historical words of Buddha. Over time, these interpretations became more clearly defined, and sentiment grew among the liberal monks to make a formal separation from the conservative Elders.

The liberal groups proposed an explanation for how their ideas were authentic Buddhist doctrine. They said that while the Hinayana sutras were being codified at the First Council, another assembly of monks hid a number of new, more progressive sutras for safekeeping. Five centuries later, these hidden sutras were rediscovered and brought forth as the Mahayana scriptures.

Much like King Asoka, who championed the older form of Buddhism, King Kanishka (78-103 C.E.), a conqueror from northern India, helped to spread the new Buddhism with passionate zeal. He called a council of five hundred monks and collected their new texts into a group. They called their new form Mahayana, the Great Vehicle, formally separating from the traditional Buddhism of the Elders, naming the older group of Buddhists Hinayana, the Lesser Vehicle. Now Mahayana Buddhists distinguished themselves as their own separate form of Buddhism.

In northwestern and southern India, Buddhism was exposed to Hellenistic influences as well as Iranian and Mediterranean cultures. The more liberal and inclusive Mahayana was open to other cultures, helping it to spread to China, Japan, Tibet, Nepal, Mongolia, and Korea.

DOCTRINAL CHANGES FROM HINAYANA TO MAHAYANA

Mahayana Buddhists developed what they considered to be an expanded, superior, and higher doctrine than that of Hinayana. The new doctrine replaced Buddha as the center and originator of Buddhism with a wider conception of Buddha. In Mahayana, Buddha, temporarily incarnated in the earthly person of Siddhartha Gautama, became Dharmakaya, the embodiment of the dharma within a succession of Buddhas over the millennia, to be followed by other Buddhas in the future. Buddha became all Being, the meaning within all phenomena, now supernatural, timeless, and spaceless. Buddha could not be found in spoken words, doctrines, or learning. The dharma body, or Dharmakaya, was transcendent, and thus Buddha's exact words and rules as memorized by Ananda and the early disciples were only a temporary embodiment, not the permanent one.

The *bodhisattva* replaced the arhat as the ideal role model. Bodhisattvas live with compassion, kindness, and patience. According to the Mahayana, wisdom is virtue, and thus being compassionate, kindly, and patient was the correct interpretation of the Buddha's teaching, not that of becoming a wise, dispassionate arhat. Bodhisattvas did not withdraw from society to find nirvana.

Their altruistic ethics encouraged good works in the interest of the whole world.

Mahayana added many long discourses on metaphysical subjects, replacing Buddha's silence in the earlier sutras. Our experience of an apparently real world, Mahayana taught, is illusion. The true nature of reality is emptiness, which is explained in the next two sections on the Madhyamika and Yogacarin Sects of Mahayana Buddhism.

The highest value was placed on what the Mahayana called *upaya*, skill in means, which meant that there were many ways to reach salvation. This allowed for a much broader repertoire of theories, techniques, and methods that could be included in Mahayana Buddhism than had been allowed in Hinayana. For example, people were permitted to worship images of Buddha with rituals, thereby finding enlightenment with faith and not simply by wisdom as in Hinayana.

Mahayana tended to be more charitable and warmer than Hinayana. Practitioners could be more emotional, personal, and interactive with other people. They produced ornate art, literature, and ritual. Hinayana continued to be more monastic, secluded, conservative, and less emotional, viewing all passions as delusions.

Mahayana now could appeal to a larger variety of situations and people. They were less strict, more inclusive with regard to women and monks of lesser attainment, as well as opening the potential for enlightenment to householders.

TWO SCHOOLS OF MAHAYANA

Two major schools of Mahayana developed with their own doctrines, called Yogacara and Madhyamika. The Yogacarin philosophy, or mind-only school, believed that our minds create reality as we experience it. The other main root, Madhyamika or middle way school, held that we cannot ever know whether reality really exists. People should remain in the middle and take neither side.

Mahayana doctrine became formalized as systems through these two schools. They would become the taproots for all later Mahayana forms of Buddhism that would be carried around the world.

NAGARJUNA AND THE MADHYAMIKA SCHOOL

Nagaljuna was a third-century Indian philosopher who founded the Madhyamika school of Buddhism. Nagarjuna's school taught philosophy as an alternative to meditation, for breaking the chains of becoming. Correct philosophical understanding is the approach to freedom from attachment, to find the Middle Way. Nagaljuna's writings led away from idealist separation from the world, and away from classical disputes in philosophy. Nagaljuna offered an alternative to the two mainstream beliefs of his time, which were the oneness of the universe and the denial of the universe.

THE FOURFOLD NEGATION LEADS TO EMPTINESS

Nagarjuna proposed a dialectic method of questioning called the Fourfold Negation. It consisted of four possible positions: (1) no position is tenable; (2) absolute versus relative existence accounts for the phenomena of existence; (3) the foundation for phenomena is emptiness; (4) codependent origination of phenomena accounts for the existence of phenomena. The Fourfold Negation can be restated as a logical paradigm, best shown in this chart:

	Is	Is Not
Is	is, is	is, is not
Is Not	is not, is	is not, is not

Nagarjuna believed that concepts were inadequate to convey the essence of enlightenment, yet concepts were still essential—that is, concepts were both inadequate and essential. Paradoxically, all four combinations of is and is not are equally possible and impossible at the same time. Recognizing that all phenomena are interconnected, no philosophical position can be taken without being refutable. Nagarjuna showed how no philosophical position can be supported without question, without bias. No ultimate certainty exists. This leaves us with only one option: emptiness, which we cannot even call emptiness without error! Emptiness is the unifying basis for all philosophies, an ultimate ground that all philosophies share.

Nagarjuna's critique of theories was neither conceptual nor cognitive because words and thoughts inevitably deceive us. Nagarjuna's approach leads to giving up thought, letting go of conceptual boundaries and definitions, indeed, of existence or nonexistence itself. By the use of thought and logic, he leads the mind of his student to recognize the futility of thought and logic. If no basis for taking a philosophical position can be conclusively demonstrated, then why take one? Madhyamika is critical of all positions, including Hinayana. This opened the way for later developments in Mahayana.

VASUBANDU, ASANGA, AND THE YOGACARIN SCHOOL

The founders of the Yogacarin movement were two brothers, Vasubandu and Asanga. They lived around 400 C.E. in northwestern India. Asanga believed in Mahayana from the start. But his brother Vasubandu began as a Hinayanan. It was while translating some Hinayana texts that Vasubandu began to find fault. He then found new inspiration in Mahayana and became a spokesman with his brother for Yogacarin.

Both brothers believed that mind is the basis for enlightenment. The Yogacarin view of the world of phenomena is that it is all in our minds. Our thoughts make the world seem real. Yogacarins used meditation to reach a state of no-thought to escape the illusion.

Vasubandu also worked out an interesting new logic. He defined an existent thing by a specific example of what it is, what it does, and then he gave an illustration of what it is like and what it is not like. He always used specifics, never general or abstract categories. For example: (1) This fireplace has a fire in it (what it is); (2) because there is smoke, there is fire (what it does); (3) so it is a wood-burning furnace (what it is like) and not a pond (what it is unlike).

This example reflects a Buddhist perspective of understanding each thing as it is in its particularity, not as a member of a class or category, as is done in Aristotelian logic. Lists of attributes are only temporary and relative. In Buddhism, abstraction is an illusion. Thus when we read Buddhist descriptions, it is puzzling from the Western perspective, where the class of something can help clarify a single individual case. From the Buddhist point of view, the class is empty, and the individual case is an example, an expression of the universal Buddha nature, which is empty of distinction. A form of logic known as Buddhist logic evolved the implications of Yogacarin further into a system.

PARAMARTHA: FINDING TRUE MIND

Paramartha (499-569) is one of the more renowned later Yogacarins who came from eastern India. He brought the school to China (546) and translated seventy-five sutras and works of Yogacarins into Chinese. He was very outgoing and traveled around the country lecturing and teaching. As a result, he gathered many devoted students who carried forth the tradition.

One hundred years later, Hiuen-tsiang (650), who was taught by one of Paramartha's students, taught Chi-k'uei (632-685), who brought Yogacara to Japan and called it the Hosso sect.

The essence of the doctrine is that defining things as real, separate objects in and of themselves is a phenomenon of consciousness. The world is an illusion, subjective—an extension of our inner conceptions. Perception can be tricked or distorted, as when we see a mirage or a conjuring illusion.

Paramartha believed that how we perceive, interpreted through language, sets up barriers to our understanding the world and the things that we are concerned about. In order to change behavior, we must change the meanings we give to things, including our dependence on language. Meaning is true essence, not the words we use. We must still the mind and withdraw from our sensory perception of the world in order to find the true Mind.

"Mind-only" is the "suchness" of an object, undifferentiated, in its true state. There are three ways to view an object. First is the imagined as real—simply itself, distinct from others. Second is the dependent aspect—how one thing is conditioned by other things. The third is that suchness or mind is the true essence of all things. In truth, there are no separate objects, and ultimately, even consciousness is illusion. Only mind exists. You can understand the truly real, or suchness, through meditation.

STOREHOUSE CONSCIOUSNESS

But the apparent constancy of phenomena and the world must be explained, and in fact was explained by the Yogacarins as *alaya*, the storehouse consciousness. Sense perceptions accumulate in a deeper core region of consciousness known as the storehouse, where they gather related perceptions, which, like a rolling snowball, produce other perceptions and conceptions that are drawn in and gather even more.

Storehouse consciousness permeates everything we experience in an all-pervasive way. For example, when you visit a clothing store, the clothes often have a perfumed smell characteristic of that store. While you are there, it affects your sense of smell. You bring an item home, and it maintains the odor for a while. The storehouse consciousness is similar, a heavy perfume that permeates everything we do and think all the time.

As a result of the storehouse consciousness, our actions, for good and bad, are affected. These actions, in turn, influence the world, which inevitably affects us, and more snowballing of perceptions and conceptions takes place. There is a feedback loop of mutual influencing, based on the storehouse consciousness. This gives constancy to our world, and makes it hard to change.

The storehouse consciousness can be dissolved by meditation. We learn to recognize the relativity of the world. Al is mind and mind is empty, without substance.

Illusion seems real, reality is illusion. Thus meditation shows the practitioner that though illusions seem real, nothing is real.

CONCLUSION

Yogacarins led their students deeply into illusion and then out of it to free them with meditation. Madhyamikans led their students with reason and philosophy and then freed them by showing them that reason and philosophy were futile. They were left with the middle way. Both schools were persuasive and effective in offering the Mahayana perspective. Each presented a part of the Mahayana whole. Subsequent development in Buddhism used their concepts as a springboard into emptiness, the foundation of Mahayana.

4
Branching Out

Form is emptiness and emptiness is form.
—Heart Sutra

BUDDHISM IS TRANSLATED INTO CHINESE

Though India was the birthplace of Buddhism, China gave Buddhism a place to develop and grow. Sutra translators and traveling monks brought the doctrine from India to China and from there it spread to Korea. Korea introduced Buddhism to Japan in 552 during the reign of Emperor Kinmei. The rulers sought concepts, rules, rituals, and principles to guide and inspire their subjects, to create order and purpose, and to help develop their lands and people. Buddhism fulfilled these purposes. The leaders patronized monks and endorsed translation centers.

Kumarajiva (344-413) was a brilliant scholar and monk who facilitated the spread of Buddhism to the Chinese—in his case through his translations of the sutras. Kumarajiva headed an official translation bureau in China where he supervised a thousand monks in the translation of ninety-four works into Chinese for his royal patron, Yao Hsing.

Kumarajiva's disciple Seng-Chao (374-414) was a student of Taoism before converting to Buddhism. He interpreted Madhyamika philosophy through Taoist lenses, and thus developed a clear and unique system of conceptualizing the inconceivable, to communicate Buddhism to the Chinese in familiar terms. Through Kumarajiva and his disciples, many Mahayana sutras were made understandable to the Chinese. Then he and his followers, especially Seng-Chao, skillfully rendered the Madhyamika and Yog-acara sutras so that these ideas, too, could continue to grow.

NEW BRANCHES GROW

The Yogacara and Madhyamika schools may have been the solid tree trunk of Mahayana. But as Mahayana took root in other countries, it grew new branches.

The first branch produced two Chinese sects, T'ien-t'ai (Tendai, Japanese) and Hua-yen (Kegon, Japanese)—both systematically classified as Buddhism. These schools held that reality can be conceptualized in certain ways. T'ien-t'ai developed a comprehensive system to reunite thinking with enlightenment. Hua-yen's grand scheme was based on intuitive sudden enlightenment over the use of reason.

A second branch produced Pure Land Buddhism, and the Japanese forms of Jodo and Shin. Pure Land made the chant the nembutsu, "Namu-amida-butsu," which loosely translated means meditate on Amitabha Buddha, into a sacred action.

According to the third branch, reality is unspeakable, unthinkable: All theories are false. Some Mahayana Buddhist sects, such as Zen, follow this tradition. Words, concepts, and theories, at best, only point toward the truth, but language cannot express it. Ludwig Wittgenstein, a renown European philosopher, stated it well: "Beyond this is silence."

A fourth branch rejected the direct use of reasoning to lead to truth in favor of other ways, such as mandalas and mantras. Tibetan Buddhism and other Tantric sects such as Shingon follow this mystical path, using elaborate visualizations and rituals as the means to enlightenment.

T'IEN-T' AI BUDDHISM

T'ien-t'ai began in China and was named after the mountain monastery where the master resided. Chih-i (538-597) is considered the founder of T'ien-t'ai. Although he was not its originator, he wrote, organized, and developed the concepts his teacher helped him to realize. Chih-i's formulations became the means of conceptualizing T'ien-t'ai's vision of Buddhism. He instituted concepts to systematize and incorporate the varieties of Buddhist doctrine into a unified, rational hierarchy. Each was given a place and a category.

T'ien-t'ai did not blend and synthesize all of Buddhism as one. Each retained its separate identity as a reflection of the whole.

THE THREEFOLD TRUTH

The threefold truth is the basic statement of the T'ien-t'ai doctrine. The *first truth* is that the world we think of as real is actually an illusion. We believe it is real because we experience it, but it is not real. The experienced world is empty of any lasting substance; it is transitory, an illusion given to us by our senses and mind.

The *second truth* is that this world of experience has a temporary existence. It is only partially or temporarily real. Things are real for now, due to their apparent, momentary existence. The second truth says we cannot say that nothing is present at all, for if we do, how could the senses and mind perceive things? Reality is fleeting, like a flash of light, but the flash does happen.

The *third truth* says there is something, but then asks what is it? It is not "nothing," but neither is it "something." A middle path emerges from the interaction between, a synthesis that includes them but also transcends them. This third truth is a mysterious fusion, so there is no distinction possible. Absolute mind is completely integrated with the universe. Everything is a function of the true state.

SUCHNESS: THE ULTIMATE UNITY

At the highest level of understanding, in a grand synthesis, all are present in one thought. This one thought is what the T'ien-t'ai calls *Suchness*, the ultimate category. Everything is just as it is.

For example, consider the common food product butter. Different kinds of butter vary in their subtle flavors, depending upon the brand, whether salt has been added, and how it is manufactured. But in its essence, all forms are still butter. Different flavors might taste differently to different people, but ultimately all butter is of the same essence.

This world is real. There is no other. The phenomena we see and experience are a function of their conditions, causes and effects, nature, and substance, which *are* intimately interrelated with the inner truth of the universe.

Whether we look at the world from the absolute (nirvana) or the relative (samsara) frame of reference, it is the same at its inner core yet different in its outer expression. The core is empty. Like a doughnut, whose nature depends on the hole, both dough and hole are necessary: No whole without the hole. Similar to physics' modern theory of matter, nothing is constant; everything is always changing. Yet the central nothingness within everything is eternal and shared by all.

In the absolute sense, everything and everyone is of one root, one essence. Boundaries are only relative, depending on your point of view, always changing. When we can experience this, we can accept that things are just as they appear. We feel the interconnectedness of all reality and live our lives accordingly, in harmony, which is the true nature of reality.

THE FIVE PERIODS

As the Chinese became more knowledgeable about Buddhism, they began arranging, classifying, and systematizing sutras and doctrines. Students of Buddhism questioned how it was possible that one individual (Buddha) could have taught so many sutras, so widely, with so many apparent contradictions and inconsistencies. T'ien t'ai explained it by dividing Buddha's teachings into five periods and eight methods.

The first period was the Hua-yen or Avatamsaka. Immediately following his enlightenment (528 B.C.E.), Buddha attempted to express the wisdom through the *Avatamsaka Sutra*. But the understandings were too advanced, and so he saved this sutra for later. The second period included the early scriptures and the Four Noble Truths that made up the *Pali Canon* of Hinayana Buddhism (528-200 B.C.E.). During the third period (200 B.C.E.-100 C.E.), the basic Mahayana sutras introduced the new concepts of Mahayana Buddhism. The *Prajnaparamita Sutras of Perfect Wisdom* were the fourth period (100-200 C.E.), with the concept of emptiness and no distinctions between doctrines. The fifth period (200-600) presented the *Lotus Sutra*, with its comprehensive unity of all teachings. T'ien-t'ai believed this period represented the most profound level of understanding.

THE EIGHT METHODS

The wisdom from each period was communicated using four teaching methods and four sets of texts. The Four Methods were Sudden Enlightenment, the most sophisticated; Gradual Enlightenment, using step-by-step Vipassana insight meditation; Secret Doctrine, incorporating rituals and mysticism; and the Indeterminate, an indirect, subtle way of teaching. In the fourth method, all students thought they were being spoken to and personally addressed by the Buddha, indirectly, through symbols, gestures, and teachings.

The doctrines included many collections of Buddhist texts. First were the early procedures laid out in the *Tipitaka*. The Shared Doctrine, used by both Hinayana and Mahayana Buddhists was next. The Distinctive Doctrine explained about becoming a bodhisattva, and the Complete Doctrine, from the *Lotus Sutra*, gave the dimensions of practice for Buddhahood, where everything is unified—all things are contained in each individual thing.

The Five Periods and Eight Methods showed how all of Buddha's teachings from different times and places could be true. Buddha had used different approaches to teach people at varying levels of sophistication. T'ien-t'ai welcomed all the teachings as a diverse resource from which the students could draw, depending on their talents, capacities, and needs.

T'ien-t'ai's clear and exacting formulations were used to teach Chinese Buddhism for many centuries. Later, T'ien-t'ai was brought to Japan and became known as Tendai Buddhism. Tendai Buddhism had a long and influential effect on Japan.

HUA-YEN: ONE IN ALL PHILOSOPHY

Hua-yen Buddhism arose in the seventh and eighth centuries. Fa-Tsang (643-712) is usually considered the founder, due in part to the volume of his writings. He is said to have written over one hundred works. He systematized and created a coherent, orderly philosophy under the patronage of Empress Wu. He was also a dynamic speaker who could move audiences with his words. According to legend, once, after delivering a dynamic lecture, the earth shook! His most popular writing was the *Commentary on the Heart Sutra*, still read today by practitioners from differing sects.

Weaving the flowers of Mahayana into a beautiful garland, the works of Fa-Tsang and the other great thinkers in the lineage helped to communicate this form of Buddhism. Eventually, Hua-yen was brought to Japan where it became known as Kegon.

THE GREAT UNIFICATION

There were three important principles in Hua-yen. The *first principle*, Realms of the Whole, was a unique contribution that allowed Hua-yen to be inclusive. Hua-yen made sense of the varied sects, synthesizing them together into one whole. On the surface, the many varied teachings of Buddha might seem different, but in their essence, they are all the same. Each sect actually presents only one view of the larger panorama, the realm of dharmadhatu.

Emptiness, the *second principle*, was central to all Mahayana sects. But Huayen doctrine included form within the formlessness. Emptiness was expressed in terms of its relation to fullness. Everything, each individual object, is both mirror and reflection, reflecting all other objects, and in turn, only the reflection in another mirror from another perspective. For example, the parts of an automobile gain their meaning united as a car, but are not, in themselves, a car. In the same way, the individual parts of the universe gain their essential meaning from the universe as part of the whole.

A calm lake quietly reflects the surroundings. In perfect stillness, which is the true image and which the reflection? Without a calm lake, no image of the surroundings can be reflected. Without the surroundings, there could be no reflection in the calm lake. They come into existence together in a flash.

A person sees the lake and the reflection as an experience. The perception takes place by means of the mind of the person viewing it. Therefore, is the perception only in the mind, or is it more than mind?

The *third principle* is Totality, mutual interdependent interaction among everything. Hua-yen included reality and substance as part of the totality, the whole. Hua-yen reintroduced logic and reason as part of the enlightened reality, essential within the grand synthesis of all that is. It all depends on your point of view, your level or realm of understanding, and your frame of reference. Therefore, Hua-yen was a round doctrine, without an edge or boundary. Each part complemented the other. No one part was complete without the other. Hua-yen's perspective was not one-sided.

Each had its place, its part. Hua-yen's realm is a totality, an integrated organic whole. It was an affirming, positive philosophy that included everything as threads in the tapestry of enlightenment. There is no obstruction since everything has mutual interpenetration and mutual identity, fused in the oneness of the dharmadhatu.

Although details may vary and emphases may differ, the essence, the central principle within all systems, was identical according to Hua-yen.

PURE LAND: THE EASY PATH

Pure Land Buddhism was a Mahayana sect that evolved gradually, beginning formally in China. Inspiration came from India, from sutras composed about three hundred years after the death of Buddha called the *Pure Land Sutras*.

The school that developed in China was led by Hui-yuan (336-416), who founded the White Lotus Society, named after a lotus-covered pond near his monastery. It was this society that became the basis for the Pure Land sect in China. They retired from society to seek seclusion and live according to the dharma. The teachings from the Pure Land perspective spread throughout other sects in China. In Japan, the ideas were organized and codified by Honen (1133-1212) into Jodo Buddhism, which arose in reaction to the often demanding efforts required for Buddhist practice.

Honen was a charismatic, warm, and inclusive man who had a deep desire to attain enlightenment. Yet he found it too difficult to practice the three disciplines of precepts, meditation, and knowledge on his own. One day Honen came across writings from the Pure Land sect that taught the use of the nembutsu. Honen was overjoyed, for here was an easy way to enlightenment.

The Pure Land adherents believed that Buddha's enlightenment was timeless and spaceless, beyond the confines of his life. Enlightenment is personified as many Buddhas and bodhisattvas. The loving bodhisattva Amitabha vowed that he would refuse to be fully enlightened until all entered into nirvana. This vow committed him to altruistic and selfless devotion to others, permitting anyone to gain from him. Amitabha's great sacrifice of his own personal nirvana was for others. The merit of a positive action can be transferred to another instead of being used by the person who earned it. Therefore, Amitabha could save anyone through transferring his merit. By sincerely calling his name, saying the nembutsu "Namu-amida-butsu," he opens his paradise to anyone.

Pure Land puts faith in the power of Amitabha. Faith in "other power," *joriki*, is the preferred path of Pure Land practitioners rather than faith in one's "own power," *tariki*. Joriki is an alternative to striving by your own efforts to reach enlightenment.

Honen's student Shinran (1173-1262) developed his own sect, known as Jodo-Shin or Shin Buddhism. One of Shinran's students evolved the Pure Land doctrine of nembutsu's power to be even more pure, a complete self-contained practice that guaranteed enlightenment if wholeheartedly performed even once.

Though Honen and Shinran exclusively focused on the nembutsu as all that was necessary, followers later modified the doctrine to permit involvement in Buddhism's other practices. Many of the sects of Buddhism have now included aspects of this doctrine—especially the chanting of the nembutsu and faith in the bodhisattva ideal as personified in Amitabha—as adjuncts to Mahayana practice.

Everyone who practices, whatever their situation, may be reborn in the Buddhist paradise. This easy way to achieve peace and enlightenment is inclusive and positive toward all. No one is excluded, regardless of former misconduct, weakness, or deficit, if they faithfully practice Amitabha's vow.

This complete faith was so simple and dramatically powerful that it appealed to many. Even though Honen himself emphatically declared that nembutsu was not a form of meditation, others used it as a meditation and still do.

The Pure Land is a sentiment within the heart of Buddhist doctrine. In a sense, we are all in the Pure Land, here and now. This is our paradise if we let it become paradise.

ZEN BUDDHISM

Buddha held up a flower at Vulture Peak and smiled, communicating the spirit of enlightenment. All the monks sat solemnly, watching Buddha. Only Mahakasyapa understood, and smiled. This was the first recorded direct transmission of enlightenment, from mind to mind, without words. Zen began at this moment. Zen tradition carried the experience of enlightenment forward through twenty-eight patriarchs in India to Bodhidharma, who transmitted Zen to China. This tradition of transmitting enlightenment without using words, mind to mind, is the cornerstone of Zen and continues to the present day.

Since Zen's doctrine emphasizes the essence within sutras and rituals of Buddhism, Zen has in whole or part been integrated with many other philosophies, religions, and activities, including art, martial arts, psychotherapy, and Christianity, among others.

TRANSMISSION FROM BODHIDHARMA TO THE WORLD

Bodhidharma (440-528) traveled to China, taught monks to meditate, and also taught them martial arts to help them actively learn. Bodhidharma believed that the elaborate rituals and doctrines in Buddhism were a distraction that prevented people from recognizing that their own nature here and now is enlightenment. "To find a buddha," he said, "you have to see your nature. . . . If you don't see your nature, invoking buddhas, reciting sutras, making offerings, and keeping precepts are all useless."

Hui-neng (638-713) changed Zen by emphasizing the idea of sudden enlightenment. He is considered the founder of modern Zen. Since our mind is the buddha, we are already enlightened. There is nothing to seek, nothing to find. Meditation can help you realize this, but doing anything with intensity will have the same result. Walking, eating, sleeping—all are opportunities to practice Zen. The practice of enlightenment is interpreted in many ways, but the core, according to Zen, is meditation.

Zen evolved into various schools and branches, Soto and Rinzai in Japan, known as the Tsao-Tung and the Lin-chi lines in China, were most significant. They had different emphases, yet both carry the spirit of Zen. Soto focused on practicing clear-minded meditation, *zazen*. These practitioners deemphasized enlightenment in favor of the practice of meditation itself. They believed practice is inseparable from enlightenment rather than a path leading to it.

The Rinzai approach fervently strove for enlightenment and continually sought to deepen the experience through the practice of meditation on *koans*, stories from Zen masters that portray the enlightened mind in teaching situations.

Koans, zazen, and Zen arts evoke the open-minded inclusive awareness characteristic of Zen Buddhism. But paradoxically, in Zen, not one sutra or koan explicitly describes enlightenment, yet all illustrate it through the ultimate fusion of enlightenment with everyday life.

5
Flowers from Buddha's Garden

The world is the movie of what everything is, it is one movie, made of the same stuff throughout, belonging to nobody, which is what everything is.
—Jack Kerouac, *Scripture of the Golden Eternity*

There is a vast collection of literature that conveys the ideas and points to the experience of Buddhist enlightenment. Those that express the words of the Buddha have been collected into two separate groups: the Hinayana Pali sutras and the Mahayana Sanskrit sutras.

HINAYANA SUTRAS

The early sutras express Buddhist concepts through stories, analogies, and lectures. They portrayed the teacher, Buddha, guiding people with real-life problems and questions. These sutras expressed Buddha's ideas about impermanence, reducing desires, and developing wisdom. Throughout, they encouraged people to take the moral path to find enlightenment.

MUSTARD SEED SUTRA

One of the most well-known sutras, the *Mustard Seed Sutra* explains the very difficult philosophical concept of impermanence through a story. A mother named Kisa Gotami was grief-stricken when her young son died in childhood. Rather than face the tragedy, she carried the dead child from door to door seeking medicine to cure him. People laughed at her for trying to find a treatment for death, but one person took pity and told her to go see Buddha.

Filled with hope, she quickly sought out Buddha. The Buddha could see that in order for Kisa Gotami to accept what had happened, she needed to understand impermanence. "Go and find grains of mustard seeds," he told her, "but only from a household where no one has ever died."

She agreed and set off to find the cure she sought. But every house she visited had the same answer: Someone in the family, either a child, parent, or grandparent, had died. Gradually she began to realize the sad truth: For all people in the world, all things are impermanent.

THE DHAMMAPADA

The concepts of Buddhism were expressed in many sutras. As more and more people wanted to learn about Buddhism, teachers gathered the insights together into a single teaching sutra that expressed the essentials. The *Dharmapada* (Sanskrit) brought many lessons together by theme into one sutra. The words were ascribed to Buddha, taken directly from his many sermons. There were a number of different versions of the *Dharmapada*, depending upon which sect collected them, but the same ideas were common to all.

The *Dharmapada* emphasizes that the only path away from suffering and toward happiness is through personal efforts. "Rouse thyself by thyself, examine thyself by thyself.

Buddha's argument to stop doing what you should not and do what you should was not based just on moral grounds, it was also pragmatic. He believed that wrongdoing brings suffering and discomfort to the doer. "Fools of poor understanding have themselves for their greatest enemies, for they do evil deeds which bear bitter fruits."

Buddha did not simply ask people to stop engaging in negative conduct, he urged them to engage in conduct that was positive. Acting with love and compassion brings true happiness and fulfillment. Most of us are well-intentioned, but we find it difficult to follow through. Buddha provided a method to tame the mind and take control of action by awakening to enlightenment. With this awakening comes the happiness of nirvana.

BUDDHA'S FAREWELL SERMON

As Buddha felt himself slipping into death, he exerted a strong effort and brought himself back long enough to speak to his students. "I am old now," he told them. "My journey is ending. But even though my body ceases to be, you have what you need within." His most famous words were "Be a lamp unto yourselves . . . seek salvation alone in the truth." Thus, in this sutra, Buddha left his disciples with the wisdom of Buddhism. Salvation comes from delving deeply into your own awareness, exploring your thoughts, feelings, and sensations. Only by holding steadfastly to the light of truth shed by your own lamp can you end suffering to find peace and happiness.

MAHAYANA SUTRAS

Mahayana Sutras reflect improvements, developments, and insights from Buddhist practice: wordless insight of enlightenment, the bodhisattvas ideal, ultimate emptiness, interpenetration of all things, and faith.

These works, like all sutras, were written as the words of the Buddha. The Mahayana legend was that immediately following Buddha's enlightenment, he preached the doctrines of these sutras. However, no one could understand the message. So he decided to begin with a simpler doctrine and save the deeper sutras for later, when people would be better able to receive more sophisticated teachings. Thus, the Hinayana sutras were taught in order to prepare Buddha's followers for Mahayana.

PERFECT WISDOM SUTRAS

The group of teachings, known as the *Prajnaparamita, Perfect Wis-*

dom Sutras, marks the new path of Mahayana. Perfect wisdom is not easy to grasp. It lies beyond descriptions and cannot be thought about. "Where there is no perception, appellation, conception, or conventional expression, there one speaks of 'perfect wisdom.'"

Perfect wisdom is quiet, empty, goal-less, and nonexistent. This definition might seem contrary to the usual conception of wisdom in our fact-hungry, data-crunching world. But the sutras explain how the enlightened perspective has a calling beyond everyday concerns, though affecting them.

The *Heart Sutra*, one of the most famous sutras of the *Prajnaparamita*, describes the relationship between emptiness and everything in our world. The sutra states that form is emptiness and emptiness is form. Everything we know and experience in the world is without lasting substance even though it exists to us in the moment of experience. When we accept ultimate emptiness and grasp the transitory nature of our existence, we comprehend the Buddhist logic of freedom. Most Zen sects chant the words of the *Heart Sutra* daily to help clear their minds of thought, opening the way to enlightenment.

The *Diamond Sutra* (*Diamond Cutter*) is another key sutra in the *Prajnaparamita*. A diamond is the hardest stone and can cut through all others, but when polished, it shines brilliantly. Like the diamond, this sutra cuts away our limited, small-minded, everyday perspective and allows us to discover a shining light—the all-encompassing wisdom of enlightenment. As Saint Paul said, "The things that are seen are temporal; the things that are unseen are eternal."

The *Diamond Sutra* makes a number of points that seem paradoxical at first, such as enlightenment is perfect wisdom. It states that there is nothing to attain and nothing to grasp, but that we must devote ourselves to trying to attain and grasp it. If we are to experience enlightenment, the sutra says we must develop "A pure, lucid mind, not depending upon sound, flavor, touch, odor, or any quality . . . a mind that alights upon nothing whatsoever." If nothing is there, how can wisdom be grasped? Wisdom is not found in objects of any kind, neither in the outer world nor of thought itself. People should recognize this truth and reject illusion. We should look for the enlightened truth of perfect wisdom in going about our lives with a clear, calm mind.

AVATAMSAKA SUTRA

The *Avatamsaka Sutra* (Hua-yen) is another large collection of sutras that were embraced and developed by the Hua-yen school in China between the first and fourth centuries. The name "Avatamsaka" means "garland" or "wreath," and this collection is sometimes referred to as the *Flower Garland Sutra*. It is known to us through Chinese translations ranging in size from forty to eighty parts of 30,000 lines total. The sixty-book translation done by Buddhabhadra (418-421) was used by the Hua-yen school to guide their path.

The *Avatamsaka Sutra* combines the understandings from the two earlier Mahayana schools: Madhyamika and Yogacarin. From Madhyamika, the sutra embraced emptiness as the ultimate nature of all things. From Yogacarin, it adopted the mind-only perspective that all being is illusion.

Integration, known as the "All in one and one in all" doctrine, is a unique contribution of this sutra. All things contain reflections of everything else, nothing exists without background and boundaries. So on the absolute level there is no distinct separation between things. Thus there is no separation between all that we actually experience in everyday life and transcendent enlightenment. Each thing relates with everything else. They coexist, all merge into one. This idea was difficult for people to understand. Fa-Tsang, the most important patriarch of Hua-yen, used an ingenious demonstration to explain the theory to Empress Wu, a great patron of Buddhism. One day, the empress said to Fa-Tsang,

"I am struggling with the idea of totality. Sometimes I feel as if I almost grasp it, but then other times I'm not sure again. Can you give me a clear illustration?" Fa-Tsang promised he would.

A few days later he returned and said, "Your demonstration is ready. Follow me? He led her to a small room where he had attached mirrors to the floor, ceiling, and all four walls. While she was watching, he placed a statue of Buddha at the center. Suddenly, the empress could see Buddhas appear, infinitely reflected in every direction. "How marvelous!" she exclaimed, as the concepts became real for her. She could literally see how all was reflected in everything else, all exhibiting Buddha everywhere. She could also see how things were codependent, all coming into being simultaneously at the moment that Fa-Tsang placed the statue down on the floor in the middle of the room of mirrors.

The *Avatamsaka Sutra* illustrates in many forms how all beings, objects, moments, and places merge, uniting with one another while retaining individuality, in emptiness.

VIMALAKIRTI SUTRA

The *Vimalakirti* is one of the most popular Mahayana sutras. Based on the insights of a wealthy businessman named Vimalakirti, who attained Buddhist enlightenment, this sutra shows how anyone can be enlightened. A person did not have to give up his everyday life and become a monk, as the earlier doctrine required.

Vimalakirti was a living example of this. His successful career showed how a person could express the silence of enlightenment even in the midst of activity, that meditation was not something separate. As he explained to Sariputra, one of the monks of Buddha's inner circle, "To sit is not necessarily to meditate. . . . Not to abandon the way of the teaching and yet to go about one's business as usual in the world, that is meditation."

Awakened living is what Vimalakirti urged. People do not have to avoid problems or challenges; from an enlightened perspective, difficulties do not have to cause anxiety and suffering. "Not to cut [off] disturbances and yet to enter nirvana, that is meditation." Sitting quietly in meditation to empty the mind of all disturbances is unnecessary. Enlightenment is a part of everyday life.

The *Vimalakirti Sutra* illustrates how enlightenment is both filled with potential and yet empty. One day, Vimalakirti went to bed, sick. A large assembly of Buddhist monks were planning to visit him. Sariputra, who had arrived early, asked Vimalakirti, "How can this small room possibly accommodate all the hosts of monks who want to visit you?"

Vimalakirti answered, "Are you here to seek chairs or Dharma?" The sutra goes on to say that one hundred thousand celestial chairs were brought in, and when all the thousands had assembled, it was not at all crowded. Vimalakirti explained that such a miracle was possible because enlightenment is filled with potential, unbounded by space and time.

When Manjusri, the bodhisattva of wisdom, arrived at Vimalakirti's bedside along with the group of bodhisattvas, he asked them all, "What does nonduality mean?"

Each in turn stepped forward to offer intellectual explanations. One said that nonduality was the resolution of opposites. Another claimed it was purity versus impurity. Finally, Vimalakirti was asked to give his insights on the subject. In response, Vimalakirti sat silently. Manjursi applauded the answer. "Well done, well done," he said. "Ultimately not to have any letters or words, this is indeed to enter into the doctrine of nonduality." Zen Buddhism followed this emphasis on wordless, unspeakable, indescribable enlightenment. Silence can be a path to follow. The sutra encourages stillness in one's house. Everyday life flows from this enlightened silence, bringing happiness and fulfillment.

LANKAVATARA SUTRA

The *Lankavatara Sutra* is one of the most psychological of Mahayana sutras. Originating around the second or third century C.E., this sutra was basic to Yogacara. It describes the mental changes that take place as an individual travels the path to enlightenment. One of the key points is that enlightenment comes when a person realizes how his or her mind influences perception. At that point, the person sees through illusion.

The following parable from the sutra illustrates this idea. King Ravana asked the bodhisattva Mahamati to explain Buddha's enlightenment experience. Suddenly, the king noticed that his home was ornately decorated. Then it seemed to multiply into infinite numbers of lavishly decorated palaces with Mahamati sitting in front of each one asking Buddha to describe his inner experience. Next, the king heard one hundred thousand delicate voices answering. Then, as suddenly as it appeared, the entire scene vanished, and the king found himself standing alone in his palace. Confused, he said, "Am I dreaming?" Then he realized that just like the images he had imagined, everything is a creation of the mind. Upon that thought he seemed to hear voices say, "Well you have reflected Oh king! You should conduct yourself according to this view."

Meditation is recommended to help people clear their consciousness of illusions. The sutra describes four *dhyanas* (meditations) to take the practitioner from beginning mental skills to fully enlightened self-realization. Through these meditations, a change in thinking takes place until illusion dispels and enlightenment develops.

LOTUS SUTRA

The *Lotus of the Good Law* (*Saddharmapundarika*), one of the central sutras for the T'ien-t'ai school in China and Tendai and Nichirin schools of Japan, was composed around the first century C.E.. This sutra vividly portrays the Mahayana conception of the Buddha, who is described as more than the mortal man Gautama Siddhartha, who found enlightenment; Buddha is the living expression of all enlightened beings, from infinite time—past, present, and future.

The sutra begins on Vulture Peak where Buddha meditates. He is surrounded by many gods, people, and bodhisattvas. The peak is illuminated by rays emanating from Buddha, and the hillside is strewn with beautiful flowers. This scene paints a new picture of Buddha, as an all-wise being with great powers and vision. Buddhist artists often used this sutra as inspiration. The sutra clearly describes Buddha's new status: "The true Tathagata, the embodiment of cosmic truth, neither is born nor dies, but lives and works from eternity to eternity."

SKILLFUL MEANS

The sutra explains why Buddhism seems to offer many different ways to find enlightenment through the concept of skillful means. When Buddha was teaching, he always tried to make each lesson relevant to the student. He recognized that people differ in their personalities, needs, motivations, and intelligence. Thus his lessons could sound very different, depending on whom he was teaching. This parable was included in the sutra to illustrate skillful means.

A father stood outside his home watching in horror as it became engulfed in flames. He knew that his three young children were playing happily inside, but realized that there was not enough time for him to run inside and carry each one out. The only way to save them all was to get them to come out themselves. Knowing how much they loved carts, he called to them, "Children, come quickly. I have a beautiful cart outside for each of you. Come see!" The children ran out laughing, full of excitement to see the pretty carts. The father did have some carts to give them, so each child was not only saved but also happy. Like the father, Buddha promises something to motivate everyone to let go of a limited perspective and seek enlightenment.

The sutra goes on to show how Buddha's teachings are like rain showering down on all varieties of plants. Water is made of one constant substance, but each plant receives nourishment from the rain in whatever way it needs. Buddha's many lectures contained Buddhist wisdom, dharma, to help people in a variety of ways, depending upon what was best for each individual.

So the nature of Dharma always exists for the weal of the world, and it refreshes by this Dharma the entire world, and then, refreshed, just like the plants, the world will burst forth into blossoms.

PURE LAND SUTRA

Faith and devotion are expressed strongly in the *Sukhavativyuha*, or *Pure Land Sutra*. The Pure Land sect (Shin and Jodo in Japan) as well as the Tendai sect adopted deep faith as a viable pathway to enlightenment.

The pure land is the paradise world of the Buddha Amitabha. The land is filled with radiant colors, jeweled mountains, fragrant aromas, and harmonious sounds. Everyone there experiences peaceful calm.

No evil can exist in this place, only the happiness that comes from an enlightened state of mind. Enlightenment allows all the inhabitants to practice goodness. Everyone is welcome here. All that is required is absolute faith in the Buddha.

The sutra reassures people that if they truly have faith, they will take on the best qualities of enlightened beings. Their minds will become pure, filled with feelings of compassion and love. Deep understanding develops out of faith and devotion to the Buddha presence—an eternal spiritual essence.

PART II
Buddhist Themes

Time's separate moments
Let objects seem
In truth, even this
Is only a dream
—C. Alexander Simpkins

The path of Buddhism takes us on a journey of inner awakening. Time and space are dimensions of the illusion of objective reality. We believe objects exist when we can locate them in time and space. But reality changes every moment. When we see beyond the obvious, perception clears and awareness opens in the deepest recesses of our being.

The themes of Buddhism must be personally discovered and felt, not just comprehended intellectually. As you continue your journey into Buddhism, allow yourself to explore these themes deeply. Then you will find yourself questioning and understanding yourself from a new perspective and open to possibilities that will improve the quality of your life.

6

The Four Noble Truths and the Eightfold Path

If one man conquer in battle a thousand times a thousand men, and if another conquer himself, he is the greatest of conquerors.
—Buddha

Although Buddhism is divided into many differing sects and schools, one set of themes was accepted as the starting point for all: the Four Noble Truths and the Eightfold Path. How it is interpreted and practiced today varies, but these basic premises are the foundation.

Buddha's original quest was to find a solution to a condition he believed was central to all human beings: suffering. The doctrine of the Four Noble Truths is Buddha's diagnosis and prescription for treating human suffering and finding true happiness. "He compared life and passion to disease—human life, like a diseased body, requires a cure by a proper regimen."

TRUTH ONE: LIFE IS SUFFERING

Life is fraught with dukkha, which is translated most literally as suffering. The true meaning of dukkha, though, is much broader and encompasses our existential condition. Buddha took a ruthless look at the inevitabilities of life and determined that we are all on a no-exit path to death. The years pass quickly, and even though there are happy moments, the good times never endure. Thus the first step on the Buddhist Path is to recognize and face that life, when looked at with raw realism, is suffering. These are Buddha's words explaining this idea:

Birth is attended with pain, decay is painful, disease is painful, death is painful. Union with the unpleasant is painful, painful is separation from the pleasant, and any craving that is unsatisfied, that too is painful.

At first glance, Buddha's description of life seems to be an example of negative thinking. But Buddha viewed suffering as the starting point, not the conclusion. He first made what he considered a realistic diagnosis of the human condition and then proceeded to offer a definite set of treatments.

TRUTH TWO: THE ROOT OF SUFFERING

Buddha's second Noble Truth is that there is a root of suffering: *tanha*, which translates literally as desires. Buddha is not advocating the end of all desires; he is talking here about egocentric desires, based on an incorrect way of viewing ourselves and our world, that bring about suffering. The more we seek to gratify our own ego, the more constricting and demanding the ego becomes.

Attempting to acquire and hold on to things is like trying to grasp and hold air in your hand. Life is impermanent. The world in which we are living is constantly changing. No one can stop the inevitable flow of time. Buddha believed that our self-centered desires can never be fulfilled, and we inevitably will be frustrated.

TRUTH THREE: YOU CAN END SUFFERING

Suffering is the doorway to deeper insight. Understanding that we can transcend suffering is the third truth. This requires an inner transformation. Through a kind of awakening we can comprehend the truth, just as Buddha saw it, and become enlightened.

TRUTH FOUR: THE EIGHTFOLD PATH

The fourth truth sets out a course of action to put an end to suffering. Called the Eightfold Path, it guides people to resolve their difficulties, find freedom from suffering, and discover happiness and fulfillment in enlightenment.

"Right Views" is the first step on the Path. "Right views will be the torch to light his way." To begin an inner transformation, people must first orient themselves. They do this by introducing themselves to what lies ahead. Psychotherapy research at Johns Hopkins University Hospital found that giving people right views about psychotherapy helped them do better with their treatment. The researchers had their best results when subjects were given an introductory interview to help them understand what their real problem was and what the treatment would involve. This "role induction interview," as the researchers called it, helped raise clients' hopes for cures and set them in the right direction.

The first steps introduce people to the right views offered by the Noble Truths. They learn that there is hope for change, since many of their problems are actually illusions they have created themselves. Life will be better when you point yourself in the right direction—by following the Eightfold Path.

"Right Intention" is the second step. "Right aims will be his guide." To seriously contemplate taking Buddha's cure, people must feel in their heart that this is what they want to do. Harold Greenwald, a renown therapist of the 1980s who created Direct Decision Therapy, believed that in order to get over problems, people need to make the decision to do so on a very fundamental level. This commitment begins the process of change. Buddhism asks not only that people make the decision, but that they also promise to do their best to persevere along the journey.

"Right Speech" is number three. We are ready to enter the process. "Right Words will be his dwelling place along the road." We begin to practice Buddhism by turning our attention to ourselves and noticing what we say. If you have ever listened to yourself on a recording, you were probably somewhat surprised by how you sounded and what you said. Observe and listen to what you say, and you can begin to know yourself.

Just listening, though, is not enough. People should be aware when they speak with malice, and try to understand why they did so. When people gossip about a friend, for example, they are being defensive, alienated from their deeper, purer being. By questioning why they said something negative, they begin to uncover their deeper motivations. Continued awareness and self-examination can help you communicate more positively, in harmony with your true nature. Right speech is an essential step along the path to change.

"Right Conduct" is the fourth step on the path. "His gait will be straight for it is right behavior." Just as practitioners observe their speech to become aware of their motivations, they must also pay close attention to their conduct. When people begin to pay attention to what they do, they may be surprised to learn that many of their actions occur unconsciously. Sometimes habits are helpful, like driving a car or tying shoelaces. But at other times, unconscious action can get one into trouble. Recognizing the difference begins with observation. Buddha believed that when people do the right thing and live according to right conduct, their suffering diminishes.

Next, reflect on these observations and ask yourself what motivated this action. Buddhists try not to be motivated by ego and instead open their hearts to caring about the welfare of others, the path of the bodhisattva.

"Right Livelihood" is the fifth step on the path. "His refreshments will be the right way of earning his livelihood." When people consider how they spend their lives, most will recognize that they spend a lot of time working. Buddha believed that because work occupies so many hours of the day, people should not hope to find inner peace if they are engaged in an occupation that is contrary to Buddhist values. Buddha asks everyone to examine their work and make sure it is compatible with an enlightened life.

"Right Effort" is the sixth step. "Right effort will be his steps." Buddha believed that when people make efforts in the right direction, positive changes begin to take place. But if they try for the wrong things, they are following a path that will inevitably lead to unhappiness and suffering. Buddha encouraged his followers to put themselves into what he called wholesome efforts—such as helping others—and to avoid unwholesome efforts—things that involve greed and crime. If you always make the correct efforts, you will eventually succeed. "Earnest among the thoughtless, awake among the sleepers, the wise man advances like a racer, leaving the hack behind."

Right effort also means correct pacing. Marathon runners know not to start out too fast. They must pace themselves correctly in the beginning; if they don't, they may find themselves out of energy before they reach the halfway mark. Similarly, becoming so deeply aware of every word and act can be taxing, even disturbing at times. Buddha encouraged his followers not to overexert themselves before they were ready. Be diligent, but always be in accord with your personal readiness.

"Right Thought" is the seventh step. "Right thoughts [will be] his breath." Correct thinking is as important to life as breathing. Buddha's primary objective was to overcome ignorance. But change cannot happen until people gain control of their minds, using awareness. "It is good to tame the mind, which is difficult to hold in, flighty, rushing wherever it listeth; a tamed mind brings happiness." Awareness continues to be a primary tool in psychotherapy today. Gestalt therapy founder Fritz Perls liked to tell his patients, "Awareness is curative."

If people pay attention to each thought, feeling, and sensation, they begin to notice how fleeting and transitory these experiences are. The concrete sense people have of themselves is merely a series of experiences that seem to blend together into one. In reality, the ego is nothing more than this series of experiences. The idea of a fixed ego is an illusion. Once people recognize this, they can begin to engage in Right Thought, to see life as it truly is. Suffering disappears. The mind becomes calm.

"Right Concentration" is the eighth and final step. Right concentration "obtains a sense of freedom, of knowledge immediate and unbounded, which sees the whole world spread below like a clear pool in which every fish and pebble is visible." In this stage, the practitioner puts all the skills built up along the path into the practice of meditation, just as Buddha found enlightenment by meditating under the bodhi tree. Then, like a knife that has been recently sharpened, the meditator's concentrated awareness cuts through illusion to perceive the world directly. Buddhists believe that direct perception is not only possible but true. As Buddha said, "He who orders his life aright passes beyond the transitory and gains the Real, the highest fruit. And when he has gained that, he has realized Nirvana." Once enlightened, suffering is no more.

7
Buddhist Psychology: Awakening from the Dream

What we call "I" is just a swinging door which
moves when we inhale and exhale.
—Shunryu Suzuki, Soto Zen master

Like modern-day psychologists, Buddha developed a sophisticated view of consciousness that included perception, emotions, and motivation—typical topics of study in psychology today. The mind not only holds answers to existential questions about ourselves and our world, but it is also the key to overcoming the everyday problems of living.

SENSE PERCEPTION

Buddha distinguished six senses: the traditional five—sight, hearing, smell, taste, touch—plus the mind, a sixth sense. Each sense has its own awareness. As Buddha explained:

The element of eye, of visible object, of eye awareness;
The element of ear, of sound, of ear awareness;
The element of nose, of odor, of nose awareness;
The element of tongue, of taste, of tongue awareness;
The element of body, of tangibles, of body awareness;
The element of mind, of ideas, of mind awareness.

We experience the world through our sensory awareness. All

the data we receive from our senses bring about a response in our consciousness. Modern psychology describes the connection between consciousness and the senses as a close interaction, with the stimulus (S), taken in by the senses, followed by the response (R), which is processed by the consciousness and referred to as the organism (0). Sensory stimuli and the related response is affected by consciousness in an S-0-R relationship. Buddha believed that the S-0-R interaction is so intimately interconnected that without sensory stimuli to be aware of there is no consciousness or response. Consciousness is always consciousness of something.

Buddha extended this even further when he said that consciousness is actually *caused* by stimuli. Without any stimuli, consciousness ceases to be. Consciousness and the sensory world need each other to exist. A sensory deprivation tank can demonstrate that we need varied experiences. After a number of hours with only minimal stimulation, subjects lose touch with everyday reality, hallucinate, and slip into an altered state. Our experience of reality is partly a function of our senses and perceptual processes. Without a world to experience, there is no consciousness.

THE CHAIN OF BECOMING

Early Buddhism proposed a theory of motivation that helped to explain how people become unhappy in their lives. As Gordon Allport, a famous psychologist, once said, "Motivation is the 'go' of personality." In a sense, Buddha would have agreed.

Perception is an active process, involving both objective and subjective experience. The sensations we have from contact with the world lead to a desire to fill our wants. We desire pleasant sensations to continue and unpleasant ones to stop. These desires bring about a desiring state of mind, which leads to grasping after things to satisfy the desire, creating a grasping state of mind. Such thoughts can lead us into difficulty. False beliefs and assumptions create states of mind that bias and limit our perception. Buddha expressed this idea:

What one feels one perceives; what one perceives one reasons about; what one reasons about obsesses one; what obsesses one is the origin of a number of concepts and obsessions which assail a man.

At the moment something is perceived, Buddha believed that ego also appears. For example, a tennis player who evaluates how he is doing as he swings the racquet will likely interfere with the shot. The thoughts about the self are what lead to difficulty, not the flowing act of correctly swinging the racquet.

Just as a fire is different according to the kind of fuel. . . . Do ye see, bhikhus, that this is [something that has] become? Do ye see that the becoming is according to the stimulus? Do ye see that if the stimulus ceases, then that which has become ceases.

The world as we know it is in a continual rhythm between coming into existence and passing away. Every event is the result of a cause that brings about other results, acting in a chain.

At first, this chain might seem to bind us to a bleak fate: If everything is determined by this logic, bound for misery, what can we hope for? Buddha painted a grim picture for the unenlightened, but he firmly believed there was hope: The path of enlightenment. People can change their destiny. Through self-awareness gained from study and meditation, people can break the chain of causation and become free to re-create their lives in an atmosphere of infinite possibilities.

NON-EGO

Buddha argued that a real and lasting ego is not possible because consciousness is ever changing along with the content. What we call our self, our ego, is in flux. "But that which is called mind, thought, or consciousness, day and night keeps perishing as one thing and springing up as another."

Any sense of an ego is only an apparent unity created by the mind. Westerners find this difficult to accept as true. But the non-ego perspective taken in Buddhism is a means to let go of mistaken ideas about self. Clarify perceptions about the ego and it becomes transparent; you see right through it. A luminous window opens through which you can see the world as it is. You make a perceptual shift that allows you to recognize that you are not just your concept of self.

MAHAYANA EMPTIES THE SELF FURTHER

The later Mahayana reinterpreted the idea of non-ego to mean emptiness. Whether or not our ego matters is not as important as recognizing that our real nature is empty. Mahayanans see stimulus-response as the moment-to-moment experience that happens in the here and now. Buddhism encourages staying with pure experiencing, not to make objects of things nor of oneself. Our true nature is filled with open potential, transcendent expression of absolute process.

This passage, from one of the Mahayana sutras, shows the importance of emptiness.

When the Mind is disturbed the multiplicity of things is produced; when the Mind is quieted the multiplicity of things disappears. In spite of defilement the Mind is eternal, clear, pure, and not subject to transformation

We are freed from the chains of false ideas about ourselves and the world that binds us to suffering when we experience the emptiness of consciousness reflected in our everyday world. "It is through absolute emptiness that Bodhisattvas, practicing perfect wisdom, cleanse the road to the knowledge of all modes."

8

Nirvana: A New Experience

If they only realized it, they are already in the
Tathagata's Nirvana, for, in Noble Wisdom,
all things are in Nirvana from the beginning."
—The Nirvana Sutra

If relief from suffering seems negative, is there nothing positive in life to seek? Is everything merely illusion, or is something more to be found in our lives? Buddhism offers the hope of something better. A different view of life appears on the horizon of consciousness. A new way to experience is born that enhances the ability to cope with suffering, even transcend it: nirvana.

What is this new experience? What makes it so different, so unique that the impossible becomes possible, the unsolvable can be solved? The answer is found in Buddhism's unique logic.

We have a long tradition in the West of problem-solving that is based in scientific reasoning and Aristotelian logic. Our culture is firmly rooted on this basis. An object or situation exists or does not exist. Cause leads to effect, premises lead to conclusions. For example, I am sitting in a chair, writing. From the usual perspective, this chair is solid and belongs to a certain class or category: a hand-crafted modern chair. We believe we understand an object when we can define and classify it in a category. We take this for granted. We can describe the chair to others. They know what to do with it—sit in it—as with all members of the category chairs. And as the renowned philosopher Bertrand Russell explained, a category is not a member of itself. So I do not sit on the category chairs, an abstraction. I am sitting on this particular handcrafted chair. It is an actual chair, an object, not an abstraction.

But Buddhist doctrine suggests that when we classify and reason about chairs in this way, we are perceiving our thoughts, not the real world. We think we know an object by its category, but we do not. We only know the category. We could sit on a desk, on the floor, or on the ground.

A wonderful experience awaits us when we free ourselves from the limitations of our categories. Since all are chairs, there is no chair! The category chairs is an illusion. Anything can be a chair when we sit in meditation.

Problems occur when consciousness attempts to grasp a situation with a narrow, limiting perspective. Enlightenment promises to liberate us from these confines, to allow us to use more of our potential.

LIFE IS CHANGE

Nothing is able to exist for more than a fraction of time. We look at ourselves in the mirror today and feel an identity, but soon we grow old. We change. We may discuss our views, asserting "This is what I think, really, and this is who and what I am." But a year from now, or ten years from now, will we still think the same? Or do we change our views as we travel through the developmental stages of life? At one point in history, no one believed that people could fly. Yet today, anyone can fly using an airplane. Computers and the internet make a worldwide linkage possible. But even as recently as the mid-twentieth century few people could imagine technology's possibilities. The problem is that we believe these temporary assumptions are true for all time, and in so doing, we limit ourselves.

Each moment of each experience is complete. When we can appreciate and embrace the goodness of each moment, suffering can be transcended and positive potential can be discovered.

ENLIGHTENED NATURE

Buddhism assures us that we share enlightened nature. All worldly objects and beings have the same inner nature at their core. Sharing this nature in common, nothing or no one can be separated from anything or anyone else. This is what is meant by saying we all have buddha-mind or that everyday life is enlightening. From this foundation, this fundamental nature that we all share in, everything we think and do, literally, *is* enlightenment.

Zen master Dogen told his students that practice is enlightenment. Practice of meditation helps us to realize what is already there: the enlightened nature within. To live it compassionately is true wisdom.

NIRVANA IS FOUND IN THIS WORLD

Temporary existence is the ground, the stage on which the drama of enlightened life takes place. The light of awareness appears through the lens of nothingness, dissolving the shadows, showing us the true world.

The essential element of nirvana is found in compassionate relationships, interaction between persons and events. An intelligent, self-correcting consciousness develops in interactions with others and the world. So in a real sense, mind is world: The universe, as Buddha said, is mind, and mind is universe, in a pattern of interaction, of interrelationship. Mind cannot be separated from body or world, and yet no world or living body exists without mind.

We express nirvana with compassionate love for others as ourselves in the peaceful harmony of the Middle Way. This harmony is a pattern of meaning that is not causal, not based in space, time, or matter. Nirvana is how this is possible.

Everything is unique, perfect, just as it is, while also inseparably part of everything else. We exist in many realms, on the relative plane of being as well as the absolute, and yet both are part of each other. Without our everyday lives, jobs, relationships, and ways of play, we would not be who we are. But we are more than just that. Without enlightenment, we would have no identity, no basis for our relative existence. Each is part of the other. The Middle Way mysteriously emerges in the Oneness between.

Nirvana is beyond any possible frame of reference, transcending all boundaries. Everything is possible because nothing is possible. Each moment is new.

9

The Bodhisattva Way: Life Is Good

The human mind possesses the Buddha-nature, unobtainable from others. It can be compared to a man who has a jewel in his clothes he knows not of, or to a man who seeks after food when he has a treasure in his own storehouse.
—Surangama Sutra

ARHATS, THE HINAYANA IDEAL

Hinayana Buddhists believe that the path to discovery is a long personal journey, taken step-by-step along the Eightfold Path. Through careful, mindful self-observation, combined with inner calming, people trace the roots of their suffering and bring an end to it. This meditative discipline brings about self-control, so that they can choose to do good and reject evil. As the *Nirvana Sutra* states,

> *To avoid evil actions*
> *To do actions that are good*
> *And to purify the mind*
> *Is the essence of Buddha's teaching.*

Eventually, arhats let go of desires. They are no longer pushed and pulled by wishes and wants. Excess thought stops, suffering ends. What remains is a feeling of complete well-being, otherwise known as nirvana. This is the path for the arhat, a method of perfecting character and obtaining the freedom to be able to follow the Truth.

MAHAYANA'S PATHWAYS: THE BODHISATTVA

The arhat's journey is only for the select few who are willing to renounce everyday life for a secluded, monastic existence. Most people would like to improve themselves, but not at the expense of family and profession. They would prefer to integrate wisdom into their lifestyle. Mahayana Buddhism recognized that in order to appeal to the everyday person, another path was needed. For this reason a new ideal was created: the bodhisattva, which means enlightened (*bodhi*) being (*sattva*).

The bodhisattva offers us a role model to follow. All people have the opportunity, no matter what their shortcomings, to elevate themselves along this noble path that perfects character. For example, when you walk into a dark room, you must first turn on the light. Similarly, bodhisattvas begin with a flash of enlightenment.

Anyone can be enlightened, but once there, the process that cultivates the experience is gradual by degrees. Through intense study, meditation, and correct practice, a person evolves this first glimmer of insight. In time, one overcomes the negative qualities within to become wise and compassionate.

Bodhisattvas do not allow themselves to attain nirvana and then sit back and enjoy their enlightenment. This would be a negative passion. Instead, they turn away from the potentially self-centered, secluded life of an enlightened arhat and devote themselves to improving everyday life by helping others. For example, if you find something wonderful, do you keep it for yourself or share it with others? The bodhisattva choice would always be to share. The bodhisattva path is an altruistic one. Instead of seeking personal enlightenment, they seek supreme enlightenment by guiding others to enlightenment.

FOLLOWING THE BUDDHIST VIRTUES

First, the bodhisattva makes four vows: (1) to save all beings, (2) to not indulge in negative passions, (3) to learn the Truth, (4) to teach the Truth to others, leading them to enlightenment.

Bodhisattvas attempt to perfect themselves according to *paramitas*, perfect virtues. Ten virtues give them definite criteria for aligning their personal ideals to those of Buddhism.

Originally there were only six paramitas: generosity (*dana*), morality (*sila*), patience (*ksanti*), effort (*virya*), and meditation (*dhyana*), culminating in intuitive wisdom (*prajna*). Later, four more were added: skillful means (*upaya*), resolution (*pranidhaina*), strength (*bald*), and knowledge (*jhana*). As in the Eightfold Path, bodhisattvas fill their consciousness with pure thoughts, practicing meditation that helps to keep their minds clearly attuned to this intent. Practice helps to perfect a virtuous life. Thus bodhisattvas train themselves by expanding wisdom and knowledge while also developing compassion and love.

Living in tune with the paramitas has its rewards, and the *Dasabhumika Sutra* (part of the *Avatamsaka Sutras*) describes the benefits as ten stages: joy, immaculate, illuminating, radiant, meditation, turned toward, going far, steadfast, sharing, and cloud of the law. According to this sutra, all who wholeheartedly practice the paramitas will feel happy. Even if you are not perfect in your practice, you will progress if you are sincere in your efforts.

THE BODHISATTVA TRANSFORMATION

In following the vows they make, bodhisattvas embrace selflessness. Concerns of the ego become of less consequence. Bodhisattvas are free from fear, worry, and insecurity because they have let go of ego concerns, such as concern over reputation, comparing themselves to others, judging their accomplishments. As we begin to let go of illusory concerns, we can focus on what really matters.

Eventually, all the efforts in living well, meditation, and good works bring about a transformation in the personality: the wish to help others. The bodhisattva can intuitively reach out to someone in a way that will make sense to that individual by using skillful means. Bodhisattvas have appeared in the world as people from all walks of life, illustrating how wisdom may sometimes be found in unexpected places.

Our hypnosis teacher, Milton H. Erickson, was a master of skillful means in the service of his patients. He specialized in helping people who had failed to get help from other therapists. Erickson believed that the helper must start from patients' own understandings and utilize their resources to help them help themselves. One patient came to Erickson because he had never been able to write. Erickson said to him, "You may not be able to write words or letters, but can you make a line?"

The patient answered, "Yes, I can draw a line."

Then Erickson said, "Can you draw a circle?"

The patient answered, "Yes, I can draw a circle."

"Well then," said Erickson, "you already know how to write. Just put the line and the circle together, with some parts going above the line and some parts going below the line. Then you have the letter *b*, or *p*, or *d*." He went on to show the patient that, by using what he already knew, he could write the entire alphabet (Erickson 1978).

Like the man who thought he did not know how to write, most of us do not realize that we can be enlightened. The bodhisattva meets people where they are and helps them to understand Buddhist truths starting with the understandings they already have.

Bodhisattvas develop the ability to determine their actions. In Zen arts, enlightenment is expressed directly as will in action. The calligrapher can control the exact moment the brush meets the paper to create a perfect stroke. There is no separation between thought and action.

Sometimes circumstances present barriers to positive action. For example, some students will say, "I have to cheat if I want to get a high grade because everyone else cheats." The bodhisattva response is to stick by one's principles regardless. Bodhisattvas develop the inner strength to make the wise and compassionate choice no matter what the circumstances.

FINDING YOUR PATH

The bodhisattva follows a path that casts personal concerns within a larger context. When you accept a bodhisattva orientation, your life takes on greater meaning, transforming a small, ego-centered existence into one that enhances all existence.

Since nirvana and this world are united, there is no need to run away from your life. You do not lose nirvana by turning back to help others. All are part of the oneness. Many doctrines become one doctrine that you learn by doing. Living well brings happiness to you as well as to those you help.

Sincerely perfect your own character in action to be kind to others, not just a select few. This is the way of the bodhisattva. As the Zen Buddhist Mumon said, "The gate is wide open and nothing blocks your way."

PART III
Living Buddhism

Sand, breeze, and sun
Join with primeval sea
To synthesize as one
Experience of unity
—C. Alexander Simpkins

The sea of Buddhism is vast and deep, yet you must search within to discover it. Everything you do reflects the wisdom of Buddha, as every drop of water is a drop of the same essence as the waters of the ocean. Draw your inspiration from the same wellspring that has nourished generations of buddhas and bodhisattvas. Now, plunge into your inner nature, a nature shared by all. With this experience comes a wonderful sense of unity, well-being, and calm.

10
Meditation:
Beginning with Your Own Mind

It is the readiness of the mind that is wisdom.
—Shunryu Suzuki, Soto Zen master

Wisdom begins with awareness, and awareness can be enhanced with meditation. Meditation will help you gain both the control and release of mental processes, leading to your own understanding of enlightenment.

There are two distinct types of meditation, each offering a pathway to enlightenment: dhyana, meditation to clear the mind; and prajna, meditation to fill the mind. The two methods are best performed in conjunction with each other. The Lotus Sutra states this principle of needing two forms:

> *The Buddha while dwelling in Mahayana used the transcendental power of the dhyana and prajna which he had realized to liberate living beings from birth and death. . . . The practice of dhyana alone, while wisdom is disregarded [causes] stupidity, and the practice of wisdom (prajna) alone, while dhyana is disregarded, causes infatuation.*

The T'ien t'ai patriarch Chih-i taught that the meditative practice of clearing the mind should be balanced by filling the mind in equal proportions. He said, "This twin realization is like the wheels of a cart and the two wings of a bird. Partial practice of them is wrong."

We offer several variations of each technique, drawn from many Buddhist traditions. You will find some methods of meditation easier than others. Experiment with the different forms and notice your reactions. Allow time for your skills to develop. Choose the variation that works best for you, or do them all.

GETTING STARTED

Pick a time when you will be undisturbed for at least five minutes. You will no doubt increase the duration of your meditation later; what is most important now is that you begin to do it. In today's fast-paced world, people often feel they just don't have enough time to fit meditating into their schedules, but most of us can find a few free minutes here and there.

Find a relatively quiet place. At first sounds may be distracting; later, you won't notice them. Many people have a room or an area set aside for meditation. Having a meditation corner may in fact help you to get in the mood. You might burn pleasant-smelling incense, hang a picture of Buddha or another inspiring image on the wall, or place a statue nearby. All of these are optional enhancements. Keep in mind that the essential component is you and your willingness to try.

Meditation is traditionally done sitting on the floor, perhaps on a meditation pillow If you are able to sit comfortably on the floor, do so. If not, sit on a low bench or in a chair. Where and exactly how you sit should not interfere with your meditation. Buddha did not believe in taking a restrictive meditation posture. Be comfortable. Sit cross-legged or in a half-lotus position (one foot is brought up to rest on the other leg).

There are several classic ways to hold your hands. One is to sit with one hand resting palm up on the other in your lap, thumbs lightly touching. Another is to let each hand rest comfortably on each knee, palms down. A third position is to rest your hands on your legs, palm up with the thumb and index finger touching.

DHYANA: MEDITATIONS TO CLEAR THE MIND

The untrained mind jumps from thought to thought, often causing a seesaw of emotional reactions. A calm mind can perceive clearly and is capable of flexibly coping with life's inevitable challenges. You can learn to tame the "monkey mind" by practicing these three forms of dhyana.

Dhyana: Clearing the Mind Meditation 1

Begin your meditation by concentrating on your breathing. Close your eyes. Sit upright so that your breathing passages are free and open, but do not strain. Allow yourself to relax and breathe normally. Focus your attention on breathing, in and out. Give one count to each complete breathing cycle, inhale and exhale. Continue to breathe normally and count up to ten, then return to one and count again. Do this for several minutes the first time. Gradually increase the time until you can sit comfortably for increments of fifteen minutes. Meditating in this manner each day can have a calming effect.

Dhyana: Clearing the Mind Meditation 2

Pick something—a statue, a vase, a picture—as an object of concentration. You can also use any ordinary household object. We have done this meditation using such varied items as a soda can, a blade of grass, and a mural on the wall.

Place the object before you. Sit comfortably and focus all your attention on it. Try not to think about anything else. Notice everything about the object—its colors, texture, features, shape. After several minutes, close your eyes and visualize the object in your mind. Picture it as vividly as possible. Keep your attention focused on the image in your memory. Whether you see it vividly or vaguely does not matter. The important point is to stay focused on it.

Open your eyes and look again. Do you notice things that you did not see before? Close your eyes and again picture the object in your mind. Is the image different now?

If you find yourself distracted by another thought, gently bring your attention back to the object. Keep returning to your focus whenever your attention wanders. Eventually, you will be able to focus without becoming distracted.

Dhyana: Clearing the Mind Meditation 3

Now that you have practiced focusing your attention, you can experiment with letting your focus go. Imagine that your mind is like a stream flowing down a mountain. Your thoughts are the branches and leaves that are being carried downstream. You are standing on the shore, watching. Can you let the branches and leaves flow past without stopping them? Can you stay on the shore, quietly watching? Let the flow of your thoughts go by. Do not identify with any one thing. Gradually, less branches float past. The stream clears. Stay with the clarity, quietly meditating.

When you are ready to stop these meditations, open your eyes and notice how you feel. Are you calm? Do your visual perceptions seem bright? Enjoy the clarity and calmness.

PRAJNA: FILLING THE MIND MEDITATIONS

Prajna meditations teach how to fill the mind with moment-to-moment experiencing. These meditations allow people to discover Buddhist concepts for themselves. Through direct observation of their own thinking processes, people come to understand impermanence, and these understandings become a springboard for letting go of cravings and desires. If you carefully watch your thoughts, you will have your own personal experience of these truths. Keep your mind open and try for yourself!

Prajna: Filling the Mind Meditation 1

Sit quietly. Close your eyes at first to lessen any distracting stimuli. Turn your attention to your breathing once again, but this time you will meditate on it in a different manner. Instead of counting your breaths, focus your attention on the process of breathing. As you draw air in, notice how the air fills your lungs and causes your rib cage to expand. Follow the air as you push it out and it exits through your nose.

Notice how each breath, in and out, is a unique experience. Even though a new breath follows immediately, each breath is a separate action. We call the process "breathing," but that is only a conceptual abstraction. If you really pay close attention, you will observe and feel the air going in though your nose and down into your lungs as your rib cage expands. Then the air goes back up through your nose and out as your rib cage contracts. This full breath is really a series of separate actions repeated over and over. Nothing more is present. Follow each breath in and out; try to become aware of how the breath comes into being and then is gone. Stay in the absolute now with each new breath.

Prajna: Filling the Mind Meditation 2

Sit quietly with your eyes closed and pay attention to your sensations. Notice each one as it occurs. For example, suppose you hear the sound of a car passing outside. Pay attention to how the sound comes and then disappears. Try not to think about it. Simply notice. Observe the sound but do not let yourself start thinking further about it—perhaps wondering what kind of car it is, how many people are in it, and so on. Just recognize the sound. Then try to notice how the sound comes and then goes. Keep following each experience as it appears and disappears. Pay attention to this coming and going of sensations, noticing their transitory nature.

Prajna: Filling the Mind Meditation 3

When you are able to follow your sensations while sitting quietly with eyes closed, try to expand your awareness even farther. Open your eyes and notice your experience as you did before. Try to stay aware of each experience, but always let go when it ends. Do not conceptualize, judge, or add to it in any way. In other words, refrain from thoughts such as "This is a nice feeling," or "I hate when that happens!" or "I hope that will happen again."

Prajna in Action 1

Expand your practice of prajna meditation even more by paying attention to every waking action, no matter how commonplace. The *Vimalakirti Sutra* encourages meditation in action. You do not have to withdraw to meditate: Enlightenment is here and now. Practice the earlier meditations until you feel comfortable with them. Then try this exercise.

Pick a small task you need to do, such as washing the dishes or washing the car. As you begin, turn your full attention to the task. Notice every aspect of the experience; the feeling of the soapy water, the cloth moving along the surface, the smell of the suds, the sound of the water. Keep noticing each sensation as it occurs. Try not to think about anything beyond the direct experience. Bring your thoughts back from any associations that carry you away from your experience. Stay focused until you are completely finished.

Once you are able to do this meditation on a single, time-limited task, try to extend your meditation over a longer period, perhaps for an hour or an entire afternoon.

Prajna in Action 2

You have probably had a time in your life when you were so involved in what you were doing that for that moment, you let go of your ego. With meditation, you can deliberately forget your limited self to find your deeper true self, your buddha nature.

Pick an activity that you find fulfilling and meaningful. Perhaps it is playing a musical instrument, practicing a martial art, fixing something, or making something. Engage in the activity as fully as you can. Let go of any ego concerns: Do not think about how well you are doing, whether you are progressing, or what other people might think. Simply do the action fully. Afterward, you will notice a pleasant feeling of relief, calm, or inner satisfaction.

EMPTINESS MEDITATIONS: PRAJNA AND DHYANA AS ONE

Once you realize the impermanence of the world and the ego, you open yourself to emptiness. With practice, dhyana and prajna meditations blend together in the wisdom of emptiness, a spiritual sense of Oneness that can transform you. The next series of meditations will guide you toward the enlightened perspective.

Empty Thought

Enlightenment does not ultimately rest on analytical reasoning. You must move beyond rational thought. Ask yourself, "Can I let go of distinctions and simply experience without analysis or judgment?" Like experiencing something for the very first time, before you have built up expectations about how it will or should be, can you simply experience this moment? Pose the question and then sit quietly. Stay with each moment and wait for your answer.

Hua-yen Totality Meditation: One in All and All in One

This meditation draws upon Hua-yen's concept of totality. Sit quietly. Think about how one thing is the boundary for another. For example, our skin forms a boundary with the air; our skin cells enter the atmosphere and the air penetrates our skin. Another example is the interaction between plants and the earth. Think about other possibilities. Now take one of these ideas and extend it outward. How does the root of the plant interact with the earth? How is the earth connected to the atmosphere? Keep expanding until you can conceive of the entire universe in one, all-inclusive single thought. Meditate on this.

Zen Meditation: Discovering Your Buddha Nature Here and Now

You do not have to go anywhere else for enlightenment; it can be found here, now. According to Zen, enlightenment is in every moment. All forms of meditation dissolve into one form, in the Absolute Now. Sit upright. Eyes can be closed or kept half open. Sit quietly until your breathing becomes steady and calm. Do not think about anything. If a thought arises, take note of it and then dismiss it. If you feel a sensation, take note of it and then dismiss it. Continually return to full attention. As Dogen said, "If you practice in this way for a long time, you will forget attachments and concentration will come naturally. That is the art of zazen. Zazen is the Dharma gate of great rest and joy!" Observe each moment with focused awareness, as if for the first time.

Nembutsu Meditation

If you find it difficult to meditate, you might like to try the "easy way" to enlightenment, nembutsu. Repeat the name of the bodhisattva Amitabha: "Namu-amida-butsu." Think of nothing else. Repeat the words often.

BODHISATTVA COMPASSION: PERFORMING GOOD DEEDS

The highest form of meditation for the bodhisattva involves helping others without thinking of oneself or receiving anything in return—this has traditionally been part of the practice. You can turn compassionately to the world with positive action. Pick something positive that matters to you—for example, volunteering at a local nursing home, becoming a big sister or brother, participating in a community cleanup. Make the time for it. Perform each moment mindfully and fully. When complete, let go of it, and continue on to something else.

If you have experimented with the meditations in this chapter, you have felt Buddhism for yourself. In meditation, sitting quietly, focusing with awareness or engaged in selfless action, you can experience enlightenment.

11

Paradise Now: Action Is Thought

Everything harmonizes with me which is
harmonious to Thee, oh Universe.
—Marcus Aurelius

Buddhist doctrine expressed what science now confirms, that everything is interrelated. As the *Avatamsaka Sutra* tells us, each grain of sand contains the ten thousand things. Like the ripples from a pebble thrown into a quiet pond, anything we do reverberates through the entire world.

People, their situation, and their reactions are in a flowing unity. Your positive actions make a difference. Your actions affect others. Consider what you do and how you do it. What you do becomes your input into the world's system. You can affect the world in many positive ways.

ENVIRONMENT IS ONE

The housekeeping of our planet requires an inner as well as an
outer aspect of ecological consciousness.
—Tucker & Williams, *Buddhism and Ecology*

Modern biological theory recognizes that everything is interrelated in an ecosystem—that is, all species depend upon each other. Scientists have come to think of this mutual interdependence as the web of life. "Much as the strands of silk in a spider's web bind one segment to another, feeding and other interactions bind all organisms to one another." Biologists arrived at this conclusion through careful empirical observation. Similar to our modern scientific method, Buddhism uses mindful observation as the method to discern the true nature of the world.

DEVELOPING YOUR SENSE OF UNITY

When we are in touch with our true mind, we naturally feel more respectful of all life as we respect ourselves. The motivation comes from within as a deeply felt understanding, not from an external "you should." According to humanistic psychologist Abraham Maslow, when we are in tune with our true inner nature, we will want to do what is best. "These are situations in which, so to speak, head and heart, rational and nonrational speak the same language, in which our impulses lead us in a wise direction."

LIVING IN ENLIGHTENMENT

After you become aware that there is no separation between you and your world, you may notice things that others overlook. Senses and nerves are magnified. You become more sensitive to addressing the perceived needs of your environment as they truly are for you. Marcus Aurelius's insight at the opening of this chapter encourages us to take the harmony of the world around us seriously: seek harmony without to find harmony within.

EXPANDING YOUR BOUNDARIES

One great splitting of the whole universe into two halves is made by each of us, and for each of us almost all the interest goes to one of the halves, but we all draw the line of division between them in a different place. When I say that we all call the two halves by the same names, and that those names are "me" and "not me" respectively, it will at once be seen what I mean.

—William James

As you become open to a larger perspective, awareness extends. When you look at a tree, you can experience the tree as it truly is. There is a blending between you and the tree. As Dogen said, "Delusion is seeing all things from the perspective of self. Enlightenment is seeing the self from the perspective of the myriad things of the universe."

You become more sensitive as your perspective expands to include the object of your perception. You develop empathy, not just with other people but with all living things. For example, in Zen flower arranging, the practitioner communes with the flower nature. Deep calm and comfort are obtained by allowing consciousness to dissolve into an experience of Oneness with nature.

Earth Meditation

We have done this exercise with many students, and they have often found that it helped them to experience their interconnection with the earth. Go outside and sit on the ground. Place your hands palm down on the land. Close your eyes. Sense the massive earth below you. Do you feel a pulsing from the activity of all who share this earth as their support? Allow yourself to notice what you perceive.

When you become more aware, you may sometimes sense events taking form before they quite happen. This can be useful. A black belt martial artist trained his awareness for many years. One day he was sitting in the front passenger seat as his friend drove. The martial artist said, "Slow down!" Mystified, his friend complied and decelerated the car. Then he asked, "Why did you say that?" Suddenly a car darted out across the intersection they were about to enter. He smiled as his friend sighed in relief, "Thanks! How did you know that?" "I don't know," the martial artist answered. "I just felt it was important to slow down just then." He had no idea how he knew, but the timely sensing was there.

One with Nature Meditation

Find a peaceful place outdoors. It could be a local park, a beach, or your own garden. Before you begin, sit quietly for several minutes and become aware of your breathing, then focus on what you are experiencing, including your awareness of the environment. Once your thoughts have settled, begin walking around. Let your attention to your experience include your surroundings as you walk. Be aware of all that you see, hear, smell, and feel. Do not conceptualize about it. Can you permit the boundaries to merge and feel your Oneness with the world?

ABILITY TO RESPOND

No separation between you and your environment also means no obstruction to positive actions. There need be no hesitation. Nothing stands in your way but yourself. Heroes respond directly to a need. "I was there," a common phrase. "I saw what needed to be done, so I did it!" Without hesitation or thought, these courageous people let go of the boundaries between self and other. They perceived a situation where someone or something needed help, and before they even thought about it, the action was done. We can all be heroes by helping in small ways, by responding to what is there.

Responsiveness Meditation

Start small, with one of your house plants. Read up on plants to learn about their needs. Then bring your plant near and meditate on it. Notice everything about it: the color of the leaves, the quality of the soil, whether it grows straight or tilted, and anything else you observe. As you observe mindfully, you may begin to sense what needs to be done. You feel for the plant as a fellow living being. If your plant is dry, provide water. If dust has built up on the leaves, clean them. If the leaves are yellow, add fertilizer. As your awareness increases, you will feel a spontaneous response. Let yourself attend to the plant as needed.

After you have been successful with one thing, expand. Try to become more aware of your environment with direct awareness. Allow yourself to respond appropriately based on mindful experiencing.

Practice mindfulness of your environment wherever you are. You do not have to deliberately think of Oneness; simply feel it naturally. What's important is the attitude; after that, correct action flows. You can express these values in your own way, respecting your world just as you respect yourself. As you travel the Path, you will find your own ways to help your world thrive.

NO DISTINCTIONS

> *In the mysterious Oneness of the universe,*
> *None is better,*
> *None is worse.*
> **—C. Alexander Simpkins**

Rise above duality to make no distinctions. Do not take sides and say "This is good. That is bad." When we think about our environment, we should always be aware of not favoring one thing over another. Everything has a place in the web of life. For example, we often think of insects as something unpleasant or frightening, but some bugs help the environment. Ladybugs can be an effective solution to white flies, a tiny insect that attacks plants such as hibiscus. The ladybug is nontoxic, without the negative byproducts that a common pesticide would have. Be sensitive to the balance of nature. Recognizing the relationships between all things, your responses can be more complex and all-inclusive.

FINDING PEACE

Putting a stop to fighting is a problem that concerns our world, from entire nations to individual relationships. To be at peace with others, we must first be at peace with ourselves. In our interdependent world, peacefulness within will inevitably lead to peace with others.

Finding Inner Peace Exercise

Observe how you relate to others and how they relate to you. Are you argumentative? When your partner says something, do you disagree without even thinking?

Observe how others relate. Are they actually as argumentative as they seem? Look deep. Are other people really arguing with you or are you projecting your own hostile feelings onto them?

Do you judge yourself or other people harshly? Do you compare yourself to others? Do you feel that you are better or worse than they? Do you try to judge your neighbors' motives? From the enlightened perspective, no comparison is correct or possible. Question yourself.

Recall your meditation practice—letting go of judgments, concepts, and opinions. Feel the deeper reaction behind your annoyance or judgment. Accept yourself and accept the other person. Trust that, within, you share in the same compassionate nature. Dig until you find the quiet mind beyond anger or judgment. Allow this shared, peaceful true nature to emerge.

Peace Is Now

Sit quietly and calm your mind. Think of a place where you feel at peace. Picture it as best as you can. Try to imagine yourself there now. Allow the calm, peaceful feelings you naturally feel there to emerge.

Notice how you become calmer, here and now, even though you are not actually in this peaceful place. Enlightenment is here and now, beyond time and space. You can bring peace with you, wherever you are. The feeling comes from within. It is always present, ready to emerge, whenever you allow it. Continue to meditate, completely at peace with yourself now.

PEACEFUL SOLUTIONS

The welfare of others matters as much as your own well-being, because if someone else is suffering, somehow, it affects you, too. Thus, working things out in a mature way is a positive basis for action. Buddhism has a definite approach: Peace happens when you openly and sincerely approach your life with compassion for others as yourself.

A new creative perspective opens to you. You perceive more directly. Begin from clear awareness. Feel the reciprocal interaction with others. Recognize that the perceptions of others are just as real and correct to them as your perceptions are to you. Both sides matter equally as part of the whole. From this empathic understanding you have the basis for working out conflicts. If I hurt you, I hurt me. This is the compassionate view, in the center.

Conflict Resolution Exercise

First, face the situation as it is, moment by moment. Use your mindfulness skills to carefully observe what is happening. Do not try to conceptualize about the conflict in order to comprehend it. Do not add personal opinions or judgments. Pause and simply observe how you are behaving. An inward glance helps. How do you feel? How does the other person feel? What are you both doing?

Consider your part in the situation. What are you doing to extend or repeat the conflict? Observe your conduct as if from a distance, from the other's point of view as well as your own. For example, if you had a dispute with someone, what are you doing that continues the dispute? Is this dispute the only alternative in this situation?

Are you viewing the conflict in terms of yourself, or are you including the other person's needs as well? Expand your boundaries of self and sense the other person as if he or she were you. How do you seem from the other person's perspective? Can you imagine the needs of the other person as real to them as your own? Is there a way to come to terms together, mutually?

From this broad perspective, new, more inclusive possibilities may come to mind.

CONCLUSION

Face the present openly with awareness. Develop your world in your own way, as fully as you can. Do not create problems or obstructions for yourself or others. You do not need to hold yourself back with conflict. Develop yourself. Meditate deeply on the present and you will find a future opening up to you that is peaceful, compassionate, and filled with potential. The ripples of your actions will help create the best possible world.

12
Mindful Work

There is nothing either good or bad but thinking makes it so.
—William Shakespeare, *Hamlet*

Everyday life is enlightening. If you accept this, your approach to everything you do changes. Little things will bring happiness. Each relationship you have will be rewarding in its own way. This feeling will inevitably filter into your work. Day-to-day interactions with coworkers and projects you are doing will bring great satisfaction and joy. With deeper understanding, you will transform your time at work. As you grow as a person, the quality of your work will improve, and you will enjoy it more, too.

WORK MATTERS

Buddha considered work an important aspect of living. He believed that work could be done in harmony with the Buddhist lifestyle: He called it right livelihood. We all need to find our own way to earn a living while we contribute to society.

Buddha specified that most forms of earning a living are honorable, but jobs that involve cheating and greed are not. Any job that is in harmony with Buddhist precepts is a form of right livelihood. It is even better if the work you find helps the world as well. Think about the work you are doing and ask yourself how it relates to the world. This leaves a wide latitude for possibilities: business, law, the helping professions, engineering, architecture, construction, sales, the food industry, transportation, and many others all contribute to life in today's world and can be perfectly appropriate to the Buddhist path.

FINDING RIGHT LIVELIHOOD

Noted Buddhist activist Thich Nhat Hanh said, "The way we earn our living can be a source of peace and joy and reconciliation, or [it] can cause a lot of suffering." Work can be an opportunity for people to express themselves, but sometimes they have difficulty discovering what is best for them to do.

Ideally, your work should be an outward expression of your inner being. Generally, when you feel interested and enjoy the everyday process of doing a job, you are in the right field. There will always be unpleasant times and frustrations, but ultimately, the bad days are to be experienced rather than judged.

The best guide to your personal right livelihood comes from within, and a very good way to become aware of your inner sense is through meditation.

SENSING CORRECT LIVELIHOOD

If you are uncertain about what to do with your life, experiment mindfully with options. Put yourself into a situation where people are doing the kind of work you think you are interested in, learn what it is like and note how you feel. Do some research on the field, either from books, on the Internet, or by talking to people in the field. Notice your reaction to the research. Imagine yourself doing the work. Is this something you would be comfortable doing for long hours? Open your awareness and your path becomes clear.

MINDFUL WORK AS PRACTICE

Right livelihood is more than just your choice of work. It also involves how you bring yourself to your work. Sometimes people feel as if work is just a way to get by until the weekend, when they can have fun and truly enjoy life. But life is happening all the time, and happiness can—and should—be found in every moment.

Some people believe that the only way to be truly happy is to do nothing, to loaf. Yet even the most devout couch potato becomes restless after a while. Buddhism agrees with psychologist Albert Ellis that it is irrational to think we are happiest when we are inactive.

Zen Master Loori said, "Work is an opportunity to practice." The Buddhist way to happiness is through mindful awareness. When you open your perceptions and fully experience activity itself, you undergo a transformation. The most mundane task can become fascinating. When people are not working in their chosen field but are instead just trying to earn their livelihood they can still find opportunities to practice mindfulness. Even boring, repetitive work can be more pleasant if it is approached with mindful awareness. You may not have thought of the positive role of your work, or expanded its scope into the world as only you can.

Active Involvement Meditation

Imagine some kind of work without actually doing it, a small task. Concentrate fully on all its aspects. What is your part in it? How can you bring your own uniqueness to it? How can you do the work more fully? Allow yourself time for comprehension and insights. Then imagine yourself putting your meditation into practice.

Meditation on Action

Approach the actual small task. If you feel uncomfortable trying this exercise at work, pick a common household chore, such as cleaning out a desk drawer. Whatever the task, do it energetically. Let yourself become fascinated.

Begin with careful preparation. Set out the materials you will need: cleaners, rags, dusters, a trash bag. Ready yourself with a few minutes of meditation; clear your mind of all distractions, center your awareness in the moment.

Fully focus your attention on the job before you. Now begin your work. Try to maintain your mindful awareness. Feel, see, and think about what you are doing. If your thoughts wander, gently bring them back as you do in sitting meditation. Allow the task to inspire you. Try to learn from any intuitions you might be having. Do not hurry. Respond directly to what needs to be done. Do not judge yourself. Attend to all the details until you are finished. Then put everything away. Leave no trace. Be careful to finish completely.

Meditate again on the present moment. Sit quietly. Can you let go of cleaning and be fully present in this moment, empty of purpose, simply being here with yourself? Do you feel calm and/ or energized?

Practice approaching other tasks mindfully until you feel comfortable with the process. You may find interesting and challenging aspects that you overlooked before.

MASTERY

When you can absorb yourself fully in your work—whatever it is—you will find yourself becoming better at it. Whether your tasks involve basic manual labor or more abstract intellectual work, mindfulness is the sure road to mastery. Mindful workers become adept; a Zen master of archery, for example, can hit the mark even with his eyes closed. A master mechanic can tune an engine and diagnose problems using his senses and only simple instruments.

The way to achieve mastery is to first learn what you need to know, to set aside unnecessary thoughts, and to then focus on doing the work. Approach your work with full awareness. Stay with the task and keep your mind clear of everything else. Work without getting on an emotional roller coaster. Walk away or pause to meditate if you become frustrated, then return to your task. Be at one and mastery will come.

WORKING TOGETHER AS A TEAM

People often assume that rewards are limited. If one person gets more, others will get less, like dividing up a pizza. We can become trapped in our concepts, imprisoned by our individual tastes— some want extra cheese, others pepperoni. But everything is empty, without lasting substance, so no limitations should constrain us. We are all part of a larger whole, one that transcends us even as we create it. We can all have pizza—there is enough for everyone. Variations can be accommodated.

Although the Western perspective tends to define situations as either/or, the business or institution that can transcend "either/or" thinking will make room for everyone in the company to thrive, thereby improving each person's satisfaction and productivity.

WORKING AS ONE EXERCISE

If you are working with others, you can incorporate meditation to help enhance your group projects. Meditating together, even if only for a few minutes, can bring more cohesiveness and cooperation to a group.

Group Meditation

Gather everyone together, perhaps in a conference room before a meeting. If possible, sit in a circle either in chairs or on the floor. Ask everyone to close their eyes for two to five minutes. (You can set the timer on your watch.) Begin by asking the group to focus on clearing their minds. Explain that if another thought appears, they should let it go and return to clearing the mind. If some in your group are inexperienced in meditation, suggest that they begin by focusing on their breathing. When you meditate silently together, new possibilities may emerge that will enable your group to work together more cohesively.

Management Enhancement

If you have management responsibilities, you have probably often looked for ways to enhance the productivity and satisfaction of your workers. But have you thought about your own links with others? The smooth operation of the group is an interaction of everyone together. By guiding each person to address his or her task fully, you will find that the whole organization benefits. A united company, working harmoniously together, develops a supportive, trusting atmosphere. People will feel they can be honest with each other, supportive of one another, able to follow through on commitments. Stay open to possibilities, let go of limited assessments of others. Seek the positive potential you have together. You will undoubtedly fulfill it.

Whether working alone or in a group, opportunities will arise to be mindful. Use them. You can be mindful whether you're part of a group, leading or managing the group. Let go of evaluating the process, just be fully present for it. Your transformation can affect the others as well in a positive way. We may begin by being mindful of specific action, as in the exercises in this chapter. This opens a door to the path to follow for an overall change. If you follow that path, a transformation of your consciousness in general can take place. And if you wander off the path of mindfulness, as soon as you realize it, be aware of it. Don't judge yourself, just continue to maintain mindful moments. This will return you to the path.

13
Enlightenment Through Art

There are always new sounds to imagine, new feelings to get at. And always, there is the need to keep purifying these feelings and sounds so that we can really see what we've discovered in its pure state so that we can see more and more clearly what we are. In that way, we can give to those who listen the essence, the best of what we are. But to do that at each stage, we have to keep on cleaning the mirror.
—John Coltrane, *On Meditations*

The Heart Sutra states that form is emptiness, emptiness is form. Form is the opening to emptiness and the mirror in which formlessness may be seen. Through this opening you can enter into the arts. The medium you choose depends on your interests and talents. Artistic creation is a means of expressing enlightenment. We can learn to see reality's illusion in form's looking-glass. Then, like Alice, we can enter through the looking-glass. Form leads back to creation, to the creative, the art of the formless.

MARTIAL ARTS: ART IN MOVEMENT

Artistically designed, the martial arts hold a firm place among all art. The outstanding martial artists are those endowed with something akin to poetic imagination, critical acumen, natural piety, and spiritual insight.

Form and the basic patterns of martial arts may be used as a way to express emptiness. The practitioner is offered an opportunity to meditate with form, precision, and exactness so as to develop mind. The practitioner then becomes attuned to a deeper understanding of the art and of him- or herself.

STUDY OF FORMS

Forms and sets in kung fu, known as kata in Japanese martial arts, are patterns of movement. Exact placement of hands, balanced posture, correct concentration of attention, and spiritual intensity are central to performing well. Through forms, martial artists learn control and the application of the basics, as well as insight into the nature of the art and its solutions to situations.

The principles for studying forms can help people to master many kinds of movement arts, whether you prefer dance or sports. With forms, you learn to integrate outer precision with inner mindfulness. Apply the following exercises to whichever art you practice. Integrate the inner and outer together; fill your mind with each detail and then let go of thought to discover perfection in emptiness.

Meditation on Form

Pick a form in your martial art, a dance routine, or a particular movement in your sport, such as a tennis serve or a bench press. Sit quietly in meditation for several minutes to focus your attention. When you feel ready, do the movement slowly, keep your attention directed to what you are doing. Feel the movement. Notice your balance, your muscle tone. Are you too tight? Too loose? Be precise in the placement of each action. Repeat the movements several times with attention to detail.

Clear Mind Movement

After you have done the previous meditation, sit quietly for a moment to clear your mind of all thought. Then perform the same movements without any thought, without hesitating, unconsciously. Move quickly, precisely. Allow your training to express itself. Do not think about anything, just let the movements flow naturally.

BUDDHISM'S LINKS TO THE MARTIAL ARTS

Asian martial arts have a long tradition of descent from Bodhidharma, the founder of Zen Buddhism. Whether or not scholars agree on actual facts, Bodhidharma is still the symbol of intensity and courage. Buddhist philosophy inspires karate, kung fu, and tae kwon do at their innermost core.

Buddhist monks were also a resource for the shogun's military, called samurai, in feudal Japan. Zen monks trained the samurai in koans and meditation to enhance the speed of their reflexes and extinguish their fear of death. In Korea, monks also took up arms to help fight against oppression. As men of peace, they became adept in unarmed combat, used to defend their principles.

DEFENSE ONLY

Self-defense does not only mean defense of oneself, it also includes helping others and minimizing violence. Many of the strikes, blocks, locks, and holds found in martial arts can be applied to safely and compassionately prevent violence while preserving life. A properly applied defense can stop an aggressor's attack without causing any harm to either person.

Self-defense should be performed with control. The correct approach to a situation with the potential for aggression is to perceive what is happening but not to add to it by losing your temper or becoming afraid. The Buddhist orientation is not to engage but at the same time to face what is before you. Anger may add fuel to an aggressor and worsen a situation. Fear often has the paradoxical effect of eliciting aggression. It is a well-known fact that bullies become more aggressive with a frightened victim. Hostility does not result from strength and confidence.

The following account illustrates this point. A store clerk was arguing with an acquaintance in front of the store. The owner stepped outside, and after loudly insulting the acquaintance, demanded that he leave. The acquaintance became even more enraged at this, threw the owner to the ground, and kicked him.

A martial artist who was passing by saw what was happening and immediately intervened. Choosing not to threaten or confront the assailant with more anger, he calmly said, "You don't want to do this!" The attacker responded by trying to kick and punch the martial artist, who blocked the attacks as he continued to talk calmly to the man. "Think of the consequences. You will be arrested and go to jail for a trivial fight. This is not a good way to settle your differences."

Eventually, the man calmed down and left. His anger was diffused because the martial artist peacefully faced the situation and interjected his defense with compassion. The skill of the martial artist prevented harm to himself and further harm to others without hurting the attacker. Later, the store owner admitted that he should not have spoken to the clerk's acquaintance in such an insulting, challenging way. He had unintentionally contributed to what happened, though of course he did not merit the beating.

The martial arts of jujitsu and aikido express the spirit of harmony. They rely on staying in the center point, transforming the defender and attacker into a harmonious interaction. Thus, what one person does is reflected in the other. Aggression breaks the harmony; correct intervention restores it. Martial arts can help to neutralize aggression.

In the martial art of Simpkins Do, practitioners are taught to keep an open mind, to meet the situation as it is, not add to it and make it worse. The martial artist either deflects offensive force or extends enough force to cope with the encounter, but the practitioner always responds with compassion for the other. Compassion requires not permitting harm to oneself or the other: no attacker, no victim.

The martial artist should never initiate aggression, nor should he retreat from it. There is an old saying among martial artists: No first punch, no second punch. What this means is that the martial artist should never be the one to throw the first punch, to start a fight. But if someone has attacked, the martial artist stops the fight before a second punch can be thrown. High-level martial artists seek the peaceful solution without putting themselves or others unnecessarily at risk.

Applying Buddhism to self-defense, you know that if there is no attacker there is no need for a defender. Step outside the role and invite the aggressor to do the same. Do not engage in a duel. Experience the nameless, formless process; seek harmony and One-ness within the situation and your martial art; be at peace. Try to return others to their best possible conduct rather than engaging with their worst. Set an example of calm and restraint. It is always better when no harm takes place.

ENHANCING YOUR CREATIVITY

Creativity involves letting go of the known to create the unknown. You can discover the uncreated inspiration for your own creativity in emptiness.

Emptiness is positive, filled with potential. It is not just a desolate vacuum; it is more like the pause in breathing, between the in and out breath. The rhythm of music includes both sound and the silence between. If there is no silence, there is also no music. No notes are possible, only a steady tone that soon is not noticed. We need rhythms to experience anything. We resonate with our experiences. Without space, we can have no boundaries, no objects, no time. Your immersion in the artistic experience can become your teacher. Guided by the unknown, you make discoveries. Naomi Minkin was an artist and art teacher to the blind, the deaf, and the elderly. When she learned that she had been accepted as an art instructor for the blind, she went home and put on a blindfold—not merely for a few hours but for an entire month. While blindfolded, she tried to create some crafts. She felt textures and shapes that her eyes had not allowed her to see, and she made some surprising discoveries. Everything she tried to create without sight came out larger than it was supposed to be. With the help of her new understandings, she invented ways to compensate for that and so was able to guide her blind students to be accurate and create as they intended. By temporarily becoming blind, she learned to see as they did. This approach can be varied in many ways.

CREATIVITY AND ENLIGHTENMENT

One well-accepted model of creativity describes four stages: preparation, incubation, illumination, verification. The stage of illumination is creative enlightenment; it is here that ideas or patterns emerge. How this comes about is a mystery. Buddhism would predict this moment of enlightenment as a gift of grace, complete in itself.

In Jack Kerouac's theory of creation, drawn from his interpretation of Buddhism, spontaneity is the key, permitting and following the flow of free expression. When Kerouac wanted to create, he carefully set the stage, immersing himself in the ideas and the preparation, and then allowed his thoughts to emerge. As they formed their own patterns, he expressed them without interference.

At times, Kerouac and other beat artists performed their creative writings to audiences—with and without jazz playing in the background. The truly beat recital was spontaneous, free, and unpredictable, expressed as it was thought.

Creativity requires immersion in the true self and unity with the unknown. Creative persons continue to evolve in their understanding of what they have created. For example, we all listen to our favorite songs and come to like them as they are. Some years later in a live concert, the recording artist changes the song. Sometimes we like the new version better, but more often we prefer the original. The enlightened perspective teaches us to appreciate both versions.

Value the creative potential in each moment. Do not get stuck in any one interpretation. The song is more than its expression in a particular performance. Direct your awareness to the heart of the song, the wellspring from which individual interpretations flow.

Exercise in Preparation
Before you begin to create, engage in a period of preparation. Learn about the topic, practice techniques, look at inspirational art. Immerse yourself in what you will be doing, but do not begin until you have given yourself plenty of time to live with these preparations, to incubate.

Exercise in Creative Enlightenment
When you feel ready to create, set aside all the techniques you have acquired and allow yourself to let go of the creative act. Begin with meditation to clear your mind, then approach your work sensitively. Allow yourself to begin to create without any preconceived ideas in mind. You may surprise yourself with something new.

RELEASE FROM THE SELF
Self-surrender helps creativity. To create, you must let go, release yourself from the illusion of self toward unknown, unrealized potential. Links are begun by the artist, but then, as the painting or the poem takes on form and shape, its composition demands a change here or there. The work transcends the ego of the artist. The artist must allow this and give to the creation what is needed until the work is complete. Each creation has its own unique mini-enlightenment, in a sense. The poem, painting, or story has a unique existence as it is, and transcends its origin or personal meaning. Genuine creation means something new to each person who experiences it.

The state of deep meditation opens up creative potential. In the gap—the openness—new potential can emerge to enhance creativity. Learn to step back and fully give yourself to the situation. Let go of preconceptions and concepts. Enlightened perception shows the way; no certain or absolute concept truly exists. No concept can possibly encompass the complex mystery of life. Nothing is possible, everything is possible. The middle way is the creative way, not just conscious, not just unconscious, but somewhere in between, accepting and including both while transcending.

BUDDHIST ART

Buddhist art has always had a dual purpose, both pragmatic and evocative. This dual purpose has been present since its beginnings in many countries. During the first and second centuries, Buddhism's early recorded transmission and acceptance from India into China was by means of statues of Buddha. These statues showed Buddha sitting or standing, often wearing elaborate clothing and jewelry. The art was displayed in urban centers during ceremonies that the monks performed to inspire interest and curiosity. Once interest was aroused, Indian monks began to teach the doctrine. The Koreans followed the same procedures when they introduced Buddhism to Japan in 552 with a golden statue of Buddha as a gift.

Images of Buddha meditating, whether in sculptures or paintings, have been transmitted to every country that received Buddhism. Buddhas and famous bodhisattvas have been depicted by artists as an integral part of Buddhism to help convey an experience without words. Settings of the sutras have also been depicted in paintings and sculptures, especially the *Lotus Sutra*, where Buddha is pictured as a deity with rays of light emanating from him, seated on lotus flowers, and surrounded by followers.

Buddhist temples were built to provide a sanctuary for meditation. Unlike some of the frightening images present in Hindu temples, Buddhist temples had an atmosphere of serenity, light, and open space, with large windows to allow sunlight to enter.

They were built to invite people to feel comfortable sharing in the spirit of Buddhism.

Buddhist art evokes the viewer's potential consciousness of calm and joy. When we look at a statue of Buddha deep in meditation, we can feel complete peace of mind resonating with our own. Wassily Kandinsky (1866-1944), the father of abstract painting, believed art is like a tuning fork whose note causes resonance in the soul. Whether the creation is abstract or representational is irrelevant—resonance is the important core, the experience of art. Buddhist art resonates with the spirit of Buddhist enlightenment.

14
Psychotherapy: The Path that Heals

This pure mind, the source if everything, shines on all with the brilliance if its own perfection.
—Hsi Yun (840), Chinese Zen master

FREEDOM FROM LIMITATIONS

The Eightfold Path details a clear way to learn about yourself by examining how you speak, think, feel, and behave. Psychotherapy takes a similar course, guiding people to become aware of themselves. Buddhism can be used therapeutically to help you on your path to discovering your deeper being.

RIGHT SPEECH AS A THERAPEUTIC TOOL

Language has a powerful influence on thoughts, emotions, and subsequent conduct. Mankind points out and defines the world with language. If you use language inaccurately, you may perceive and respond inaccurately.

Derogatory language is based on judgments—for example, this person is bad or that behavior is ridiculous. Using these kinds of judgments when referring to a significant other leads to reactions that do not reflect the true nature of the situation. Distinctions such as this person is good or that person is bad lead us away from direct contact. We move farther from the real into an illusory world of abstraction. Be correct in how you use language. Do not use words that create illusions. Seek truth in the situation. Meditation can bring you back in touch.

Listening to Language Use

Listen to yourself as you speak to a person who annoys you. Does your voice sound harsh? Loud? Grating? Listen to the words you use. Are you judgmental or critical? What are you thinking as you listen to this person?

Listen to yourself as you speak to a person about whom you feel positive. Listen to the sound of your voice as you speak. Compare this to how you sounded when you spoke with the person who annoys you. Also, take note of the words you use. Is your language influencing the other person's perception of this relationship? Does your choice of words correctly express how you feel? Can you describe your feelings better?

Reviewing Relationships

Consider the Buddhist idea that all living beings share in the same nature, and that all are therefore equally united. Now think about the relationships you just observed. Are they truly as they should be? Can you appreciate and cherish others as yourself?

RIGHT THOUGHT, RIGHT ACTION

Contemporary psychotherapy models usually include restructuring patterns of thoughts and actions. Changes in our thoughts lead to changes in our feelings. The same is true of conduct. If we change our behavior, our feelings and thoughts tend to change as well. The basis for change is simpler than it seems. Behavior, feelings, and thoughts are linked together in such a way that each affects the other and each can change the other.

We create our experience by how we think and feel. If you think negative, hostile thoughts, you will feel as if the world is a hostile and negative place. Often, such thoughts are outside awareness, occurring as subvocalizing undercurrents. You can explore your inner thoughts by meditating mindfully.

Exercise: Noticing Your Inner Critic

Sit quietly and clear your mind for a few minutes. Once you feel calm, think about something that has been on your mind lately: a person or a situation. What are you telling yourself about it? Do you say things like "That person is awful" or "This is unfair"? Allow yourself to become aware of what you are telling yourself, but do not think anything about it, simply observe. When you begin to explore your inner self, it is very important that you do not judge yourself harshly. By allowing awareness, you will begin to change. Nonjudgmental mindfulness has a healing effect.

OVERCOMING STRESS

Fear, worry, and tension often accompany stress. But these emotions may be intensified by thoughts about the stress. Fear involves running away or avoiding threatening or uncomfortable situations. But what lies behind fear may be thoughts like "I can't tolerate this" or "This is scary." Worrying often involves repetitive reviewing of concerns without being aware of it. Tension can result, leading to secondary difficulties such as high blood pressure or psychosomatic ills. Do not add to your stress. Use right thinking instead.

A better attitude can help you cope with stress. Courage, as Ernest Hemingway used to say, is "grace under pressure." Buddhism offers a positive way to think about your life situation. Through meditation, you can stay aware of moment-to-moment processes, and do whatever is needed to stay relaxed. Each experience is complete. Although you cannot know for certain what will be next, nor what it will mean to you or others, you can be fully alert and attuned in the here and now. Then you can discover your resources to handle stress gracefully.

Meditation on Fear and Discomfort

Don't try to avoid stress—embrace it. Meditate on the discomfort from your stressful situation. Notice the feelings, body experiences—tightness in your stomach or shortness of breath. Accept these feelings for what they are—sensations. Notice how they change from moment to moment. Remember how each experience is impermanent, rising and falling. Pay attention to distinctions over time. Can you recognize that the discomfort is a series of experiences?

Stay with your moment-to-moment awareness. Stop imagining the future or ruminating about the past. Now is the only reality. Do not add to it with secondary assessments. Appreciate each moment of each experience as unique, without precedent.

Give yourself to your stressful situation wholeheartedly, without hoping or despairing. Simply trust in each moment's fullness and each moment's emptiness.

DISSOLVING ANGER

Anger, cravings, as well as other inner struggles can be dissolved by shifting your point of view. It is helpful to think of things from two perspectives— the relative and the absolute—and then to grasp the interrelatedness. We are individuals, yet we are also citizens of our country and citizens of the world. As the Avatamsaka and Lotus Sutras teach, we are part of the Oneness, part of each other. If I am angry with you, I am also angry with myself.

But in a real sense, what is there to be angry about? If nothing exists from the absolute perspective, we cannot be absolutely angry, only relatively. Anger from the relative perspective may seem to call for a particular action. We may want to prevent the other from doing something we don't like. We may even feel like chastising them, even if it won't resolve the situation.

From the perspective of the absolute, however, everything changes. We know that anger is a transitory emotion. We can let go of our anger and look for the compassionate solution, whatever that may be. This understanding changes how anger is experienced by reducing it to a more manageable level.

Anger also involves judgment. For example, they should not be doing this to me, or things should be different. Sometimes we wish the world were otherwise, but to insist that it should be is not a reflection of true nature. According to Buddhism, the world just is. If you can accept this, you will have a more balanced and tolerant reaction. Situations may annoy you, but they need not enrage you.

LESSENING CRAVINGS

Careful attention to each moment can bring release from compulsions and control impulses. This is the correct use of mindfulness in programs for drug and alcohol abuse. When the person becomes aware of the true nature of their situation, a middle way, a path of moderation, opens up.

Clear, mindful awareness permits control of behavior. As people become more aware, they gain a moderate perspective. By facing their actions with awareness, the path to follow for change is clear: just do the correct thing. They learn to accept responsibility for actions and their consequences. Openness gained from meditation makes it possible to learn from consequences and make better choices in the future.

Meditation for Impulse Control

If you are struggling with control of an impulse—smoking, nail-biting, an Internet addiction, excessive alcohol or drug use—you can help yourself with meditation. Practice the meditation exercises in Chapter 10 until you can comfortably follow your experience and have some success with clearing your mind. Meditate on your difficulty. Notice all the sensations and thoughts associated with it. Analyze them according to insight meditation, as distinct experiences, arising and passing away. Embrace the feelings as sensations and nothing more. Do not add your usual thoughts, which probably make you want to engage in the action. Do not do the action. After you have spent some time reflecting in this way, relax and clear your mind of thought. Repeat this meditation several times each day. Eventually, as you gain natural control of your actions, you will find your impulses weakening.

If you cannot gain control, face this and accept it. Recognize your need for help, and seek help so you can return to the path. The important thing is to follow the path of right conduct.

ACTUALIZING FROM WITHIN

We seek balance in our lives. Buddhism offers guidance in how to achieve this by following the Middle Way. One modern learning theorist has found this to be true in his research on the set point. Previous theories held by E. L. Thorndike and B. F. Skinner believed that satisfaction and reward were a continuing, positive experience that encourages behavior: More is better. Reward for behavior was thought to restore comfort. Behavior that is rewarded increases.

Timberlake found that too much reward for behavior can be discomforting and, paradoxically, unsatisfying. Buddhism's Middle Way would predict this unlikely seeming occurrence. For example, by the end of a long vacation, many people begin to feel impatient to return to work. Relaxation should be in the correct amount: not too much, not too little. As another example, if we are unrewarded for our efforts, never receiving positive feedback for what we do, we are unhappy. But if we get too much praise, even though we might theoretically like the idea, we also feel uncomfortable. We have a built-in capacity to know what is right. We seek balance.

Carl Rogers, one of the founders of humanistic therapy, believed that the capacity to instinctively know good and bad can be used to guide our conduct. This capacity is a compass for action. The source of true ethics is within. If we follow the path Buddha set out, we will act compassionately toward others as toward ourselves.

Then we will find ourselves able to help others overcome their suffering as well as our own.

Actualization is an important part of healthy, positive living. We feel good, energetic, and happy when we are fulfilling ourselves. We cope with adversity better when we trust that stress is a temporary state of affairs, part of the process of actualization.

The light of the path is within, beyond concepts and abstractions. A deep heartfelt vow to do what it takes to fulfill our worldly goals and to help others is part of developing an enlightened lifestyle. To actualize ourselves we must actualize potential in all. This is the psychological aspect of the doctrine of Mahayana, that *self*-actualization means *other*-actualization. We are one, not separable from the world. Where is the exact boundary? There is none; each requires the other. The self includes others. Begin with those for whom you care, then widen the circle.

THE FAITH THAT HEALS

Faith can evoke a positive transformation. Researchers in psychotherapy have found this, too. As one of our teachers, Jerome D. Frank, M.D., Ph.D., said, "Faith is the most precious commodity without which we should be very badly off."

Much research has been conducted to measure the effects of faith on healing. In one study, a group of patients undergoing surgery for detached retinas were given a test to measure their faith in the operation. Those who scored high on the test healed much faster than those who scored low. In a commencement speech to doctors, Frank said, "By fostering the faith that heals, we can enhance our therapeutic power, a goal towards which we all continue to strive." Faith can help you to tap resources to live a healthy, happy life. You can cultivate faith with meditation.

Faith Meditation

Meditate deeply to quiet your mind. Think about your source for strength. Feel the connection and allow yourself to draw from it. When you let go of doubts, you open yourself to new possibilities. View yourself and your health in the broader context of enlightenment and discover a harmonious integration of mind and body, society, nature, and the cosmos.

Conclusion

If you change your patterns of thought, the concepts you hold to so dearly, the world will disclose new potential to you. Though you cannot change the past, you can change the present and change the future.

Love for all beings is at the center of Buddhism and of life. Once you clear away negative, judgmental, critical thoughts, what is left? A clear mind, open to the positive potential in each moment, each situation, each person.

Peace of mind is founded on compassion, caring in a deep sense, without clinging to what has been or what must be. Enter the void with faith. Emptiness is filled with potential: May the clear light of enlightenment shine for you.

> *Eternal truths*
> *Their spectrum of light*
> *Makes shadows transparent*
> *Dissolving the night*
> —C. Alexander Simpkins

Timeline

BUDDHISM IN INDIA

563-483 B.C.E.	Siddhartha Gautama, the Buddha
528 B.C.E.	Buddha's Enlightenment
483 B.C.E.- the present	Buddhism of the Elders (Theravada, later called Hinayana)
483 B.C.E.	First Buddhist Council at Rajagriha
383 B.C.E.	Second Buddhist Council at Vaisali & dissenting Mahasangiti Council
274-236 B.C.E.	Rule of King Asoka, Great supporter of Theravada Buddhism
237 B.C.E.	Third Buddhist Council at Pataliputra & Tpitaka gathered and written in Pali
200 B.C.E.- C.E. 100	Mahayana sutras introduced and written in Sanskrit
C.E. 78-103	King Kanishka, Great supporter of Mahayana Buddhism
C.E. 200	Nagarjuna, Founder of Madhyamika School
C.E. 400	Asanga and Vasubandu, Founders of Yogacarin School

BUDDHISM SPREADS

240 B.C.E. Ceylon (now Sri Lanka) first country to receive Buddhism. Brought by Mahinda (King Asoka's son)

C.E. 100 Theravada Buddhism transmitted to Burma and Thailand from Sri Lanka

C.E. 317-372 The three kingdoms of Korea receive Buddhism from China

BUDDHISM IN CHINA

C.E. 100-400 Indian Buddhist missionaries bring Buddhism to China

C.E. 336-416 Hui-yuan, Founder of White Lotus Society, basis for Pure Land (Amida) Buddhism in China

C.E. 344-413 Kumarajiva and his bureau translates Buddhist texts into Chinese

C.E. 374-414 Seng-Chao, Kumarajiva's student and translator

C.E. 418-421 Buddhabhadra translates Avatamsaka Sutra into Chinese

C.E. 440-528 Bodhidharma, Founder of Ch'an Buddhism (Zen in Japanese)

C.E. 499-569 Paramartha brings Yogacara to China

C.E. 538-597 Chih-i, founder of T'ien-t'ai Buddhism

C.E. 638-713   Hui-neng introduces Instant Enlightenment to Zen; considered father of modern Zen Buddhism

C.E. 643-712   Fa-Tsang, Most important patriarch of Hua-yen Buddhism

BUDDHISM IN JAPAN

C.E. 552   Korea introduces Buddhism to Japan

C.E. 632-685   Chi-k'uei brings Yogacara to Japan

C.E. 800   T'ien-t'ai brought to Japan, becomes Tendai Buddhism

1133-1212   Honen founds Jodo (Pure Land, Amida Buddhism)

1141-1215   Eisai introduces Rinzai Zen to Japan

1173-1262   Shinran founds Shin Buddhism

1200-1253   Dogen introduces Soto Zen to Japan

Buddhism, Mindfulness and Meditation Resources

Meditation and Mindfulness Apps
These apps for smartphones and tablets (iOS and Android versions) are helpful for supporting one's daily mindfulness and meditation practice and connecting with worldwide practice communities. Enjoy!

The Insight Timer app supports your meditation with bells for daily practice and allows you to connect with a worldwide meditation community (https://insighttimer.com).

The Lotus Bud Mindfulness Bell offers a simple daytime reminder to mindfully awaken throughout your day (https://apps.apple.com/us/app/lotus-bud-mindfulness-bell/id502329366).

The Headspace app, featured in the *New York Times,* makes practicing simple mindfulness techniques easy (https://www.headspace.com/headspace-meditation-app).

The Mindfulness Bell app allows you to set a bell that rings randomly as a reminder to stop and breathe (https://apps.apple.com/us/app/mindfulness-bell/id380816407?mt=).

Publications
Bays, Chan Chozen. *Mindful Eating: A Guide to Rediscovering A Healthy and Joyful Relationship with Food.* Shambhala Publications, 2009.

Brach, Tara. *Radical Acceptance: Embracing Your Life with the Heart of a Buddha*. New York: Bantam, 2004.

Braza, Jerry. *Moment by Moment: The Art and Practice of Mindfulness*. Vermont: Tuttle Publishing, 1997

Braza, Jerry. *The Seeds of Love: Growing Mindful Relationships*. Vermont: Tuttle Publishing, 2011.

Busch, Charles. *Soft as Water*. Sweden: Irene Publishing, 2018.

Chodron, Pema. *When Things Fall Apart: Heart Advice for Difficult Times*. Shambhala, 2016.

Cope, Stephen. *Soul Friends: The Transforming Power of Deep Human Connection*. Hay House, 2017.

The Dalai Lama and Tutu, Desmond. *The Book of Joy: Lasting Happiness in a Changing World*. Avery, 2016.

Davis, Martha and Robbins, Elizabeth. *The Relaxation and Stress Reduction Workbook*. New Harbinger, 2019.

Delio, Illio. *The Humility of God*. Franciscan Media, 2006.

Gach, Gary. *Pause Breathe Smile*. Boulder: Sounds True, 2018.

Goleman, Daniel and Davidson, Richard. *Altered Traits: Science Reveals How Mediation Changes your Mind, Brain and Body*. Avery, 2018.

Goldstein, Joseph. *Mindfulness: A Practical Guide to Awakening*. Sounds True, 2016.

Halifax, Joan. *Standing at the Edge*. New York: Flatiron Book, 2018.

Hanh, Thich Nhat. (Series): *How to Sit, How to Love, How to Walk, How to Eat*. Parallax Press, 2014-15.

————. *Miracle of Mindfulness*. Beacon Press, 1999.

————. *Living Buddha, Living Christ*. New York: Riverhead Books, 1995.

_____. *Inside the Now*. Berkeley: Parallax Press, 2015.

_____. *True Love*. Boston: Shambhala Publications, 2004

Hanson, Rick. *Hardwiring for Happiness*. New York: Harmony, 2013.

Hanson, Rick. *The Practical Science of the Buddha's Brain*. Oakland: New Harbinger, 2009

Karas, Elaine Miller. *Building Resilience to Trauma and Community Resilience Models*. Routledge, 2015.

Kahneman, Daniel. *Thinking Fast and Slow*. FSG, 2013.

Kabat-Zinn, Jon. *Full Catastrophe Living*. Bantam, 2013.

Kornfield, Jack. *A Path with Heart: A Guide Through the Perils and Promises of Spiritual Life*. New York, Bantam, 1993.

Linehan, Marsha. *Building a Life Worth Living*. Random House, 2020.

Masters, Robert. *Bringing Your Shadow Out of the Dark*. Sounds True, 2018.

Nghiem, Sister Dang. *Mindfulness as Medicine*. Berkeley: Parallax Press, 2015.

O'Donohue, John. *Anam Cara*. Harper Collins, 1998.

O'Donohue, John. *To Bless the Space Between Us: A Book of Blessings*. Double Day, 2008.

Ostaseski, Frank. *The Five Invitations: Discovering What Death Can Teach Us About Living Fully*. Flatiron Books, 2019.

Radmacher, Mary Anne. *Lean forward into Your Life*. Conari Press, 2015.

Rohr, Richard. *Falling Upward: A Spirituality for the Two Halves of Life*. Jossey-Bass, 2011.

Salzberg, Sharon. *The Revolutionary Art of Happiness*. Shambhala Publications, 2002.

Schneider, Gary. *Ten Breaths to Happiness. Berkeley: Parallax Press, 2009*

Simpkins, C. Alexander, and Annellen M. Simpkins. 1997. *Zen Around the World*. Boston: Tuttle Publishing.

———. 1999. *Simple Zen: A Guide to Living in Balance*. Boston: Tuttle Publishing.

———. 1996. *Principles of Meditation*. Boston: Tuttle Publishing.

———. 1997. *Living Meditation*. Boston: Tuttle Publishing.

———. 1998. *Meditation from Thought to Action*. Boston: Tuttle Publishing.

Suzuki, Shunryu, *Zen Mind, Beginner's Mind*, (50th Anniversary), Shambhala Publications, 2020.

Stella, Tom, *Finding God Beyond Religion*. Skylight Paths, 2013.

Teasdale, Wayne. *The Mystic Heart*. Novato: New World Library, 2001.

Tolle, Eckhart. *The Power of Now*. Novato: The New World Library, 1999.

Van der kolk, Bessel. *The Body Keeps the Score: Brain, Mind, and Body in the Healing of Trauma*. Penguin Books, 2015.

Williams, Florence. *The Nature Fix: Why Nature Makes Us Happier, Healthier, and More Creative*. New York: Norton, 2018

"Books to Span the East and West"

Tuttle Publishing was founded in 1832 in the small New England town of Rutland, Vermont [USA]. Our core values remain as strong today as they were then—to publish best-in-class books which bring people together one page at a time. In 1948, we established a publishing office in Japan—and Tuttle is now a leader in publishing English-language books about the arts, languages and cultures of Asia. The world has become a much smaller place today and Asia's economic and cultural influence has grown. Yet the need for meaningful dialogue and information about this diverse region has never been greater. Over the past seven decades, Tuttle has published thousands of books on subjects ranging from martial arts and paper crafts to language learning and literature—and our talented authors, illustrators, designers and photographers have won many prestigious awards. We welcome you to explore the wealth of information available on Asia at www.tuttlepublishing.com.

Published by Tuttle Publishing, an imprint of Periplus Editions (HK) Ltd.

www.tuttlepublishing.com

Copyright © 2020 C. Alexander Simpkins

Library of Congress Publication Data in process

Hardcover ISBN: 978-0-8048-5261-6

Ebook ISBN: 978-1-4629-2175-1

25 24 23 22 21
10 9 8 7 6 5 4 3   2111TO

Printed in Malaysia

TUTTLE PUBLISHING® is a registered trademark of Tuttle Publishing, a division of Periplus Editions (HK) Ltd.

Distributed by

North America, Latin America & Europe
Tuttle Publishing
364 Innovation Drive
North Clarendon
VT 05759-9436 U.S.A.
Tel: 1 (802) 773-8930
Fax: 1 (802) 773-6993
info@tuttlepublishing.com
www.tuttlepublishing.com

Japan
Tuttle Publishing
Yaekari Building 3rd Floor
5-4-12 Osaki Shinagawa-ku
Tokyo 1410032, Japan
Tel: (81) 3 5437 0171
Fax: (81) 3 5437 0755
sales@tuttle.co.jp
www.tuttle.co.jp

Asia Pacific
Berkeley Books Pte. Ltd.
3 Kallang Sector, #04-01
Singapore 349278
Tel: (65) 67412178
Fax: (65) 67412179
inquiries@periplus.com.sg
www.tuttlepublishing.com